IT'S ALL MY PARENTS' FAULT

Robert Henderson

Taking Back Ownership & Control of Your Life Following Familial Trauma or Abuse

The Very Top Left
Postlagernd
1235 Wien, Austria.

Note to the reader: This book is intended as an informational guide. The remedies, approaches and techniques described herein are meant to supplement, and not be a substitute for, professional medical care or treatment. They should not be used to treat a serious ailment without prior consultation with a qualified health care professional.
ISBN 978-3-9519930-0-3 paperback
ISBN 978-3-9519930-1-0 eBook

Cover design: Jessica Bell, jessicabelldesign.com
Interior design: Amie McCracken, amiemccracken.com
Proofreading: Helen Baggott, www.helenbaggott.co.uk

To send correspondence to the author of this book, send a first-class letter to the author c/o The Very Top Left, Postlagernd, 1235 Wien, Austria, or contact the author directly at:
www.roberthenderson.at

This book is dedicated to all of you who have experienced, or who are continuing to experience adversity in your lives and are seeking a way through and out of your circumstance so you can enjoy a life of peace, happiness and fulfilment.

Contents

Acknowledgments

On earth:

To Julia Preuß, Elfi Mayr and Lea Benedejcic, thank you for all your suggestions, comments and support during the early and final drafts of this book.

To Nathalie Mayer, who behaved as a best friend should and never once let me off the hook during the whole three years of writing this book. It wouldn't be the same without you.

And, of course, to my parents, Mary Kavanagh and Brian Henderson. What a threesome we were! Let's hope that when we meet up again, in heaven or wherever, that we will be able to look back at our time together and raise a glass to life.

In heaven:

To the boys: Krishna, Buddha and Jesus Christ.

To the girls: Kwan Yin, Mother Meera, Svaté Barbory and Maria Magdalena.

Thank you for all your support and inspiration.

There's always a candle lit and a place for you at the table.

Foreword

This book is about discovering who you are. Not necessarily the person you are now, the person you find yourself to be today but your true self, the person you are actually destined to be, the *you* you chose for yourself to be on coming to this earth and about doing the things you need to do in order to become that person and to have the fulfilling life you have always wanted for yourself.

Some people are already there. Their lives have gone well from the moment they were conceived and they continue to live their lives in harmony and in alignment with the path they have chosen for themselves. Nothing has happened to blow them off course. For some people, however, things haven't been so straightforward. Through some form of circumstance or adversity, they have got pushed away from the life they wanted and now, after years of living a life that has been difficult or painful or has felt neither fulfilling or even of their own choosing, want to find and manifest a life that brings them ease, reward and happiness. This book is for you.

When we are born, we are born with a blueprint of our future life within us. This is the life we freely choose for ourselves, just before we incarnate. It is only a rough drawing of a life. It is not set in stone, as it allows us to maintain our freedom of choice while we live through it, but it does contain certain details such as the kind of general lifestyle or career we want for ourselves. The details of this life, known as our destiny or soul purpose, are held within our spiritual consciousness, the part of us that continues on after we die and which certain people such as mediums or clairvoyants see as our ghost or spirit.

The world we are born into, however, is not aware of this and nor does it keep a copy of our blueprint on record. As a newborn, we are also unable to communicate to those around us of the existence of this blueprint and the fact that we already know what we want to be in our later life. As we grow up, we also tend to lose contact with our spiritual selves and with it go the details of our destiny stored within. The process of reasoned thinking takes over. Education and employment then work to push us even further away from our true selves and towards the social collective. We get blown off course.

Over time, we can lose touch with ourselves so much so that a point comes when we get the vague feeling that either something is missing in our life or that we could be doing something better with our life. What is missing is our connection to our spiritual selves and what we could be doing better is following our own path instead of the path that has been laid out by other people for us to follow.

We can also get blown off course by the lives and actions of those around us, especially by those who are close to us, such as our immediate family. When we are born, we are unable to control the world we are born into and if that world is harsh, such as being born into an abusive or neglectful family environment, then being at the centre of our own lives and attaining the kind of life we want for ourselves gets pushed down and kept down. We can be forced to live a life that is in constant reaction to the actions of those around us. We can end up surviving instead of living. Often for many years. Sometimes, when we later marry, we can find that we are still trapped in the patterns of our childhood and that those patterns continue to keep our wishes and our desires far out of reach.

Whatever path your life may have taken you on and whatever set of life circumstances you have been born into or find yourself in, this book is here to help. This book is a guide to show you how to get your life back on track, back to the way it should be, back to the way it should always have been, back to the way you first chose it for yourself to be.

Although this book is written for everyone, large parts of it are devoted specifically to helping those who have suffered, or who are continuing to suffer some form of personal adversity and who are seeking a way through and out of that adversity. A healing of life and circumstance, whether past or present.

For ease of understanding, this book is divided into three parts:
Healing.
Realignment.
Manifestation.

Healing looks at a way to heal and move on from the past. Healing is important if you have endured some form of adversity in your life and you are now seeking a means that leads you away from that adversity and towards a happier and more fulfilling life. It is the way I took myself and therein lies its value. I know from giving workshops on healing in the power of someone standing up and sharing with others their journey of healing. If what they share is truthful and if the issues they talk about are fully resolved, the power of that sharing triggers a deep healing in those who are listening, or, as in this case, reading. It is as if when one person has come through bad times, it shows that there is a way through which empowers others to follow. Their freedom opens the door to freedom in others.

Realignment reveals how to find the life path your life should be on. This is important, because when you are trying to get your life on track or back on track, you need to know what track your life needs to be put on. Being on the wrong track or putting your life back on a wrong track can lead to unwanted and unnecessary stress that adversely impacts your life, whether emotionally, mentally, physically or spiritually.

Manifestation is divided into two parts: Preparation and Practicalities. Preparation is a list of things to check before you go off and start manifesting the fulfilling life you have always wanted for yourself. It is a bit like the mirror, signal, manoeuvre checklist you do before you pull out into a street of traffic from a kerbside parking place. If you don't follow that simple check list, when you pull your car out into the street, you might hit an obstacle. Preparation is designed to remove all possible obstacles from your path.

With nothing now in your way, Practicalities examines The Law of Attraction and Trusting the Universe before laying out a practical plan and approach to getting the life you have always wanted for yourself.

In the section on healing, this book uses my own healing journey as its source. Throughout, I make references to healing sessions I did with my teacher, which opened the way to healing my hurtful relationship with my family, in particular my mother, to client case studies from my career as a massage therapist-healer and to dreams and meditations I had and did over the fifteen-year period of 2005–2020 and from which I gained enormous insight.

At the outset, I have to say that I did not follow a traditional way to healing and fulfilment. I did not have a professionally trained therapist, doctor or life coach to guide me. I chose an esoteric way. I chose to work with an energy worker who guided me, over four years, through the emotions and energies of my hurtful past, until all emotions and energies, all memories, thoughts and resulting beliefs were revealed. Even those aspects of my past that were forgotten or hidden from me. Everything was laid out in front of me. This process of revelation brought understanding and understanding brought sufficient calm within me to be able to let go, forgive and move on. In this book, I will reveal the method this energy worker used with me to help me through. Throughout the book, I will refer to this energy worker as my teacher.

At a time when everyone wants to be healed quickly without doing any of the necessary hard work, I have a little bit of unwelcome news to impart: healing can take time. It can take time and it can take effort. This is because no one else can do all the work for you. A teacher, a guide or a healer can and certainly will help you in the beginning and along the way. They can be a part of your healing process but when they are not there with you, you have to continue the work yourself. My teacher did exercises with me that I could continue on my own after we finished working together. The good thing is, is that as you get used to doing healing exercises by yourself, you will find, in time, they get easier and easier to do. It is as if your body knows what is going to happen and likes it so much that it starts doing the healing exercise itself without you needing to push it or guide it. The process of healing, which can start out initially as a few weeks or months of hard work with your teacher, can end up being an almost effortless automatic process of self-healing which keeps going until you no longer need it.

Although I did much of my healing work on my own, I generally advise against doing it yourself. You need time to heal and if you try doing it by yourself, you need even more time. I am lucky because I have no family ties or commitments. I can lie in bed for a week or a month, waiting for some previously buried issue in my life to naturally and organically rise to the surface of my conscious awareness where I can examine it, process it, understand it and let it go. If you're living with a spouse, two children and with a full-time job, you can't do that. That is why it is better to work with someone else, a person trained in their relevant field of expertise. Working with someone else pushes the healing process along more quickly. I've been working on myself for over eighteen years. This has allowed me to experience, understand and journal each and every aspect of the hurt that not only I felt in my life but also the hurts that both of my parents experienced in theirs. This has enabled me to see everything that needs to be done when one is recovering and healing from a period of adversity and then to be able to share that wisdom in book format. I guess you could argue it is part of my soul purpose.

Throughout this book, I have tried to use as simple a language as possible in my writing. Simple words make this book easy to read, but that doesn't mean that the book is meant to be read all in one go. The words are two-dimensional but their meaning is not. Parts of this book are very detailed and contain a lot of information within a very short space, especially in the sections on healing and preparation for manifestation. The result can be quite a heavy reading experience and this is why the book is designed to be put down every few pages so it can sink in. If you read it too quickly, you miss its potential to heal, so please, read it slowly. No weekend binge-reading.

Part One.

Healing.

An introduction to healing.

Throughout my adult life, I have never felt a full connection to life, to other people and to the world around me. There has always been some kind of an invisible wall between me and everything else. It's like I can see that everything is everywhere and all around me, but somehow, I'm not actually out there and in it, being a part of it and living it. I have an intellectual understanding of life, I'm clear in that but I often find it difficult to experience or really *feel* life. Some people carry this experience in themselves for large parts of their lives. It happens when something goes badly wrong at some stage in your life. When that happens, you stop integrating. You stop integrating into your environment, into the life around you and you stop integrating yourself into your body. Instead, you go in the opposite direction. Away from your environment. Away from the life around you and away from your body. And you can do this in either one of two ways. You can retreat. Back to where you came from. Back into yourself. Into your shell. Often, into your head. Or you can escape. You push part of your consciousness away from yourself, out of your body and beyond your head where you end up living a life partially outside of yourself, in the space between the physical and the spiritual. Either way, it is how you protect yourself from what is happening around you. Of the two survival strategies, I chose the latter.

I was born unwanted. Not by design, but by accident. I was actually my mother's hope for happiness. Trapped, at a very young age, in a loveless marriage, my mother did the one thing my father never did; she took a decision and acted upon it. Unable to make her marriage work, she thought that having a child would bring her and my father together. She took inspiration from her own mother who had sacrificed her life for her children in the act of making her own marriage work. As my mother said:

Not loving myself
I grew to hope that
by sacrificing myself
I would love myself
In the same way
I loved my mother
For the way she sacrificed herself.

(From a meditation I did on the theme of sacrifice, during which the spirit of my mother came to visit me and leave me this message, 7 February 2012.)

It is a decision many women take and sometimes it works. In my mother's case, it didn't. She realised it within weeks of conceiving me and the realisation brought the prospect of her future into frightening focus.

Her life choices became suddenly very stark. She could leave her marriage and return home but that would be to a father with whom she had already had a very difficult relationship and towards whom she still carried enormous amounts of bitterness, hatred and unforgiveness. He had never loved her and if she were to return home pregnant or with a newborn child, it wouldn't be long before things would deteriorate, possibly badly. The only other option was to stay where she was. Where else could she go? She lived in a conservative, Catholic country where divorce and remarrying were denied women and where shame and guilt was the actual prevailing religion.* Trapped, at twenty-two, to a man eighteen years her senior, who, thanks to his own mother, had become terrified of women. A woman angry at men married to a man terrified of women. And now with a child on the way. The reality wasn't just frightening, it was life-threatening. Faced with such blackness ahead of her, and in absolute despair, my mother reasoned that the only way out was the way out. Suicide. She tried. Once, possibly twice. Pills. First as a tester then as the real thing. But that failed too. And so, I was born. By the time I entered this world, I was already living partially out of my body as a result of trying to escape from my mother's womb. I was born confused, lost, very afraid of what had just happened and very afraid of my mother. Unable to trust. Unable to reach out. Into a world where no one wanted to be where they were and no one wanted to face what was happening. It was in such circumstances that I lost my connection to myself, to my family and to where I was born. My roots. It happens.

(*Religion in this context = the way to control people through moral judgement.)

Of course, I never knew any of this had actually happened to me. The earliest circumstances of my life were subsequently totally hidden from me. My mother, god love her, was too ashamed to answer the questions I had for her in later life concerning the circumstances of my childhood and my father disowned himself of the whole thing as, he argued, it was not his decision to have me in the first place. By the time both my parents had passed away, I still had no idea of the circumstances of my earliest life.

Surprisingly, in the end, the only person who did know turned out to be me. My subconscious me. The me that is remembered by the body but forgotten by the mind. It was my body, from which I had lost all connection, that had all its life been trying to tell me what had happened by leaving little clues for me to solve: two hernia operations in childhood, an undescended testicle, burst appendix and finally the clue which forced me to pay attention: suffocating panic attacks in my thirties. If I hadn't then found a teacher to help me to listen to my body, I would never have been able to join those dots together, all the clues my body had been leaving me, into a single, linear map that described the course of my life up to that point in time. I would never have realised that your body retains a snapshot of every important thing that happens to you during your life and if you turn your awareness inwards into your body and examine the clues it leaves for you, every part of your life is revealed to you: your past, your present and your future. It's all there. Even the forgotten or hidden things. All the lessons you need to learn about your life are available for learning. And don't worry if you've never been aware of this and you don't know how to read your body this way, there are people here to help you. People who are trained in energy and spiritual arts, such as energy workers, light workers, spiritual healers, medical intuitives, mediums, clairvoyants, sensitives, channelers and shamans. People who, for whatever reason, can sense or see things about you that you cannot. And the reason why such people are important is that they can guide you to seeing aspects of your life which you may not yet be aware of but which may be blocking you in your desire for a better understanding of your life, in your desire to heal and let go the past and in your desire to create a better life for yourself. I refer to these people frequently throughout this book and I call them 'people trained in the spiritual arts'.

This is how this book proves its worth. This book is a guide, a guide to the pitfalls that block your way on your life path, on your way to healing yourself of your past and on your way to manifesting a brighter, happier and richer future for yourself. By revealing the pitfalls, you see what needs to be done in order to make everything go right. Where possible, I offer guidance on the ways and means to do that, but this book is not designed to do all the work for you. This book is ultimately about discovering who you are, not the person you are now, but the person you are destined to be, the *you* you chose for yourself to be on coming to this earth and about doing the things you need to do in order to become that person. Only you can do that. Not me, for I do not know who you are. I do not know the destiny you have chosen for yourself. But you do. And because you do, you already have the answers. All the answers. They are in you, held deep inside you, at your core. That is your power. That is your strength. And this book will help show you how you can get there. How you can unlock those answers within you and discover that power for yourself.

So, let's start with the section on healing in which I show you a way to heal yourself of any pain or adversity, past or present, that you may have experienced in your life.

What is healing?

Healing is doing whatever you do to help yourself overcome adversity. It can be anything from going out and having fun with your friends to get away from the stress at home to staying at home because it is safer to stay in, eating three hearty meals a day to observing a week of fasting, taking medication to practising yoga, praying for help to talking to a trained therapist, undergoing hypnosis to doing a shamanic sweat lodge. There is no wrong way. Nor is there any absolute right way either. What works for others might not work for you. What works for you might not work for others. Healing can be overcoming illness, abuse, hardship or loss, something you did to cause hurt to another, something you did to cause hurt to yourself or hurt that was caused to you by someone else. It is this latter form of adversity that this section of the book deals with. How to heal your life when you have been hurt by another.

There are as many different ways to overcome this type of hurt as there are books written about it. It is a bit like overcoming cancer. Not everyone overcomes cancer the same way. There are variables. That's why there are so many books on the subject. If there was a single way to full recovery from cancer which worked for everyone, there would only ever be one cancer recovery book. Same with recovering from hurt, whether it be emotional, mental, physical or spiritual hurt. There are variables, so there are different ways. The best I can offer, the best anyone can offer, is to share their path to recovery and to see if it resonates with anyone else. Even if that shared path to recovery doesn't fully resonate with you, the fact that another person has pulled themselves through a similar situation to yours does. It shows you it can be done. Parts of the shared healing process may resonate with you. Parts of it may inspire you to try parts of it yourself. It can show you a way through you didn't see before; a way to deal with a situation you hadn't considered before. It's like a set of fresh eyes. A different perspective. It can trigger something powerful within you; a thought, an idea, a plan, a positive. It can start working on you today, tomorrow, next week or next month. It can last days, weeks, months, years or the rest of your life. A way forward is a powerful force and reading one which has worked creates a force of power inside you.

I wish to share with you two distinct approaches to healing: a practical approach that involves working one-to-one with someone else and a more spiritual approach that combines the use of spiritual energy or the energy you can find in nature with the ideas, inspirations and information you can get in your dreams or meditations. The first approach applies to the early stages of healing, when you have to discover and examine in full what needs to be healed. The second comes after, when everything that needs to be healed has been revealed and now you have to work on letting go, forgiveness and finding yourself again. The first approach formed the basis of my first book, *Emotion and Healing in the Energy Body*, while both the first and second form the basis of this, my second book, *It's All My Parents' Fault*.

Although the two approaches to healing I wish to share are the journeys I took myself, I have opened them out for you in such a way that they can be seen as journeys you can take too. I describe the methodology of the one-to-one healing I did with my teacher in as objective a way as possible so you can understand it and evaluate it yourself. I describe in the most practical ways possible the more spiritual aspects of healing and although I cannot share with you absolutely everything about this particular way of healing yourself, such as how to interpret all your dreams, I describe enough of the process to show you that if you follow this way of healing, it works.

The Healing Process (I).

A practical approach, working one-to-one with an appropriately trained professional, teacher or guide.

Releasing the past.

You have to let go the past
So you can be free
To be here now; here today
So you can be free to be anyone, anywhere.

A key part to healing yourself and your life is to heal any major hurt that has happened to you in your past. For most of us, before we can move forward towards a healthier, happier and more fruitful life, we need to let go of the past, for it is the holding onto the past that hinders our way forward. Think of it as coming out of a supermarket clutching two of those big brown paper bags of shopping that you see in the movies and a man comes up to you with a set of keys to a brand new car and says: "They're yours if you can sign for them" and produces the car's registration slip from his pocket. How do you sign a registration slip with both of your hands full of groceries?

Healing yourself of a hurtful event from the past depends on a number of variables:

1. The size of the event.

There is a difference between moving on from a short, disappointing relationship which has just ended and moving on from an abusive childhood.

2. How much you remember of the event.

It is easier to heal a hurt you remember all the details of than it is to heal a hurt where you have forgotten much of what has happened. When you cannot remember all the facts of a hurt, it is harder to understand it and therefore harder to process and let go.

3. When it happened.

It is easier to heal a hurt that happened to you six months ago than it is to heal a hurt that happened to you in childhood. A hurt that happened to you in childhood will more than likely have triggered further hurtful events in your life which will show themselves, in retrospect, to be all interconnected. All the subsequent interconnected hurts will first need to be examined, understood and healed before the original hurt can be healed. It is like peeling the outer layers off an onion before you get to the core. A hurt that happened six months ago, on the other hand, may not have led to any subsequent hurt and therefore is easier to let go.

4. Who perpetrated the event.

It is easier to forgive an ex you were with for six months than it is to forgive one or both of your parents.

5. Is it a finished or continuing event?

It is easier to heal a hurtful event that has now finished than it is to heal one which is still happening. It is also easier to deal with the perpetrator of your hurt if they are dead than if they are alive. This is because, on communicating with the dead, through the services of a medium, for example, you discover that the dead do not lie. They are incapable of lying. They are only able to speak the truth. When you ask them a question such as "Why did you do that?", they reply truthfully. When you ask a living person "Why did you do that?", there is a chance they will lie. This does not help you with your understanding of events that you will need to understand in order for you to let them go and move on from.

Understanding everything that happened.

From the experience of letting go and moving on from my own past hurt and from the experience of helping others to let go and move on from theirs, I have found that the most important early factor in the healing process is the remembering and understanding of everything about the hurt, including the reasons the person who hurt you had for hurting you. This latter part of understanding is not always easy to uncover, but it can be done. This book will show you how. I have also found that not everyone needs to understand the whys and wherefores of their past hurts in order to move on from them, but for the most of us, the 90% of humanity, including myself, we do.

Remembering and understanding everything that happened is important. When a hurtful event happens to you, such as an act of violence perpetrated on you, your physical body absorbs some of the energy of the act into itself, where it holds it and stores it. It is a normal and natural bodily process.

Your body, however, additionally absorbs energy from the environment where the violence happened and energy from the person who acted out the violence on you. The energy you absorb from the person who acted out the violence on you includes a 'snapshot' of all the energies of their life experiences that have led them to the point of acting out that violence on you and includes the reasons, both conscious and subconscious, they had for attacking you.

Your body's behaviour of absorbing energy from past events is the reason for subsequent repeating patterns of subconscious behaviour. Repeating patterns of subconscious behaviour is your body's way of telling you that you are still reacting in the present to something from the past which you have lost memory of or to something from the past you haven't yet fully processed, understood and let go and that only by fully remembering or fully understanding that thing, will you be able to set yourself free of it and move on from it.

This is why, in later years, when you try to move on from a hurtful event, if there are still aspects of the hurt that remain undiscovered, you will find that you cannot fully move on from it. This is because your body is still holding onto the energy of those uncovered aspects of the hurt and if your body is still holding onto them, then, for your body, they are still real and they are still happening. And you cannot move on from something which, for a part of you, is still real and still happening. Your body will not let go something you have yet to uncover and your conscious mind will not set you free of a subconscious pattern of behaviour it does not understand.

It may be that you don't need any help in remembering and understanding a hurtful event in your life. It's already all there, clearly encapsulated in your mind. You are able to let it go and move on from it by yourself. Sometimes, however, you may need to ask someone to fill in some missing gaps for you, such as asking a friend of an ex if your ex ever said anything about why your relationship with them ended. From your friend's reply, you can often get the answer to a question you had about the (now finished) relationship and this answer gives you the closure, the final piece of understanding you needed in order to let it go and move on from. Sometimes you have the opportunity to talk with the person who caused you your hurt and to ask them what happened and, if possible, why it happened. This is not always easy. This person can deny, forget or lie about the hurt and often they do not understand themselves why it happened. You may then have to seek outside assistance in helping you understand what happened, such as with the services of a professionally trained therapist. If it is the case that you are no longer in contact with the person who hurt you or that the person who hurt you is no longer alive, you can get help from people trained in the ability to communicate with people who are not available for face-to-face communication, such as someone trained in energy or spiritual arts or a family constellation therapist. It is possible to remember and move on from a hurt you have mostly forgotten and to uncover the reasons for a hurt perpetrated on you by someone you are no longer in contact with or who is no longer alive.

When choosing to work with someone in the energy-spiritual arts, as I did, choose someone in the same way you would choose a doctor for your heart problem. Try to find someone with an excellent reputation and who is well established in their area of expertise. See if you know anyone else who has worked with them and seek their opinion. When you first make contact, explain exactly what kind of help you are seeking. If they say they can help, ask how. Ask them to explain the methodology they use. If they can do it, they'll be able to explain it. See if you can meet them first before choosing to work with them. Maybe suggest a thirty-minute consult. This can be done face-to-face or over the internet. Maybe they give weekend seminars from time-to-time in your area. Go along and see what they're like. See if you like the person and can get on with them. Trusting and liking the person you will work with are important.

The process of healing an emotional wound is the same for healing a physical wound.

Let's say you are out running, cycling or playing sport and you have an accident. You slip and you fall on your left knee, cutting it badly. You go to the hospital to get it cleaned and stitched up. The nurse there will probably open the wound a little so they can get into it and clean all the dirt out so there isn't any chance of infection. Then when the wound has been cleaned, it is stitched up. The stitching then knits and the wound is healed. If the wound is not fully cleaned, it will lead to infection and you will have to return to hospital to get the wound reopened, re-cleaned and re-stitched.

The same process applies to healing an emotional wound, such as having been in an abusive childhood or relationship. The wound first needs to be opened in order to be cleaned. Opening is the process of revealing all the dirt, all the hurt, everything that happened and then understanding why it all happened. Cleaning is the process of forgiving and letting go everything that happened after it has been understood. Once the whole hurt has been opened and cleaned, it can then be stitched up. The stitching then knits and the hurt is healed.

Opening and cleaning the wound.

Opening and cleaning the wound of a past emotional hurt is an incredibly enlightening experience. Yes, it's painful. Yes, it stirs up memories, but they are never as visceral as you think they are going to be and yes, it stirs up strong emotions, but the revelations you receive about your life and the life of the person(s) who hurt you, change your fundamental understanding of life completely. It becomes a process of total personal transformation. Although it is fundamental to healing, however, not everyone is ready for it.

Some people who have suffered emotional hurt in their past prefer instead to bury their hurt. They ignore it, bypass it or deny it, so when you ask them about their life they tell you that they are perfectly fine, that there's nothing wrong with them and that they don't need any help.

Some people who have suffered emotional hurt in their past can be left carrying the pain of their emotional hurt in their bodies, such as chronic abdominal-digestive pain, chronic lower back pain, heart pain, breathing difficulties, pain across the diaphragm, joint pain or even internal organ pain. Their natural assumption is that their bodily pain is medical in origin, so they seek help from their local doctor or hospital. Tests are done but come back clear. 'Nothing appears to be the matter' is the diagnosis, yet the person is still clearly in discomfort. The medical world coined the phrase non-specific body pain to describe such pain and the usual course of action to combat any medically-defined condition is to prescribe a medically-approved course of treatment, such as medication, such as steroids or painkillers.

Some people, however, try something a little extra to help them with their pain. They try an additional alternative health practice to help ease their pain, such as yoga or massage. Results can be immediate. Pain disappears. Energy levels return, stress levels drop. What can also happen, however, is that new pain appears. Pain where there was no pain before, referred pain, or an old pain resurfacing. What most people think in such circumstances is that their new pain is also physical in origin. They have overdone it in yoga and they have strained themselves. The massage was too strong and has caused them pain or discomfort. The reason looked for is always physical, yet what is happening may not be physical. It may be emotional. Underlying their initial surface physical pain is their emotional pain, the pain from the past that they have ignored, bypassed, denied or forgotten, but which their body has not. The emotional past that is causing them their current physical discomfort. And now that the massage or yoga has stripped away the top layer of physical pain, the underlying emotional pain is revealed. The wound has been presented and is now ready for opening and cleaning.

At this point some people understand what is happening. Others don't and continue with their massage or yoga practice trying to deal with their emotional pain as if it were physical pain.

Some people who understand what is happening ask if there is any way to continue their yoga practice or massage sessions without uncomfortable memories or emotions from their past coming to the surface but you cannot stop your body's natural process of healing itself once it has been triggered, even if that wasn't your original intention when you started.

Finally, there are those who realise that the only way forward is to go back. Open the wound, expose all the dirt, clean it out, then stitch it up. I was one of those people.

For my healing process, I chose to work with an energy worker, my teacher, and the methods she used with me were both simple and highly effective: the use of breath, focus, sound, awareness and perseverance.

The way she and her methods worked can be summed up quite easily.

The first time I visited my teacher was for a clairvoyant reading, a sort of life reading during which she looked into my past and saw a lot of pain. After the reading, she suggested I return after a couple of days so she could do some exercises with me to help release some of this pain. I agreed.

On entering her healing room, she sat me down in an armchair while she sat facing me on another. There was a gap of about three metres between us. She told me we were going to work on the solar plexus area of my body. She told me to close my eyes, relax and breathe normally. I did. Then she told me to gently focus my attention on my solar plexus. After a minute or two, she asked me to then focus my breath on my solar plexus and to pretend, as it were, that I was breathing in and out through an imaginary hole in the front centre of my solar plexus. So far, so good. Then she suggested I make a sound on each exhalation of my breathing, a vowel sound, such as "aaaa" or "eeee" or "oooo". When I added the vowel sound to my exhalation, it created a slight vibration in my solar plexus.

All went well for the first few minutes. I was doing everything and feeling nothing. It was easy and I was enjoying myself. After five minutes however, I started to wonder what was the point of doing an exercise in which nothing was happening.

I opened my eyes. "Nothing is happening", I said. "Just keep going" came my teacher's reply. So, I went back to my breathing and eeee-ing. Again, after a few minutes I repeated: "Still nothing happening". The same reply came back: "Keep going". By now I was beginning to get agitated, although I wasn't aware of it at the time. I began to shift in my chair, needing to do more movement than just sit, breathe and say "eeee". I was also beginning to get impatient. "Are you sure about this, because I'm not feeling anything. All I'm doing is sitting here, going eeee". Again, the gentle, but firm reply: "Keep going". Now I was getting angry. What was the point of doing something that was wasn't doing anything? The breathing and going "eeee" was now irritating me. I got up out of my chair, walked around and looked at my teacher. She looked back. "Sit down. Breathe. Eeee. Keep going". I was now doing the exercise with more resistance than willingness. I gathered myself, sighed and started again. Breathe, focus, eeee. After a further few minutes I exploded. I got up. "This is stupid", I said. "Sit back down and do the exercise", came the reply. My teacher was now making me really angry. "God, you're just like my mother", I exclaimed. Ta'daa!!!

That was it.

Yes, I had had a slight discomfort in my solar plexus before we started the exercise. Within minutes of starting the exercise, this top-layer of discomfort had been stripped away. The first layer of the onion. What lay underneath was my emotional pain, as characterised first by agitation, impatience, frustration and then anger. The second layer of the onion. Underneath the emotional layer, the cause of my emotional pain: my mother. The third layer. So, by working from the outside inwards through breath, focus, and sound, it was revealed to me that I stored an enormous amount of anger towards my mother and had been doing so for many years and that this anger was at the root of my general feelings of agitation, frustration, impatience and anger in life and was causing me physical discomfort in the area of my solar plexus and, as it later transpired, in my jaw muscles, tops of shoulders, mid-back, stomach, lower back, kidneys, navel, pelvis and sacrum. Physical, bodily pain related to my emotional relationship with my mother. I had never joined-together those two dots before. Most people don't.

I went on to repeat this method of breath, focus and sound with my teacher on almost every area of my body and each time I went through the same set of experiences: feeling uncomfortable, becoming emotional and then seeing the memory or cause of that particular discomfort and emotion. Each time I did the exercise, it revealed another piece of the jigsaw of my painful past.

My teacher first guided me to focus on areas of my body, which she later revealed to me as chakras, then on very small points on my body, which she later revealed as acupuncture points and finally on specific organs or parts of my body, such as my lungs, kidneys, liver, navel and tailbone. All in all, I worked with my teacher on a daily basis for about four months spread over four years (one month per calendar year). It was an intense experience.

The purpose of doing these exercises with my teacher was to reveal the forgotten, hidden and subconscious reasons why my life had turned out the way it had and to explain why I was the way I was behaviourally and emotionally, both in my controlled behaviours and emotions and in my uncontrolled behaviours and emotions. The former was important because things had happened in my earliest life and infancy which had been subsequently totally hidden from me and the only way to find out about them was to release the remaining emotional experiences and memories related to those events which were still stored in my body, in the area most closely related to my birth and earliest childhood; my tailbone. So, I did another set of breathing exercises with my teacher, this time focussing breath, sound and focus onto my tailbone. As always, the combination of exhalation and vowel sound caused a vibration. The vibration loosened and released the feelings, emotions and memories which had been stored in and around my tailbone since the time of my birth. This caused me first to feel and experience uncomfortable sensations and emotions, such as extreme icy coldness and deep anxiety and then, with my eyes closed, to 'see' in my mind's eye the memory of the event housed in my tailbone, a memory that revealed itself in the form of the following abstract life story:

In this lifetime (it feels like the 1700s or early 1800s) my mother is poor.

She sells sexual favours to men to keep herself alive – enough money to buy herself food.

A man, who is a wealthy landowner, becomes one of her clients.

I sense his words:

"This is our secret."

However, my mother falls pregnant.

The wealthy landowner finds out and desperate to keep his family name clean,

he kills my mother with me in her womb.

And so I die in my mother's womb.

I sense the mans' words:

"You were never meant to be born."

(These are the notes I wrote immediately after having this alpha-state dream, while working with my teacher on 25 January 2005.)

The process of turning your attention inside yourself moves your level of consciousness from a normal state of consciousness into a slightly subconscious, or unconscious state, known as an alpha state of consciousness. It is the same state as the state you experience when you are just waking up out of a dream. It is in this alpha state that you are able to see and experience your subconscious while still in a conscious state. Working with a teacher enables you to remain in this alpha state long enough for hidden details about your life, stored in your subconscious, to come into your consciousness, making you now aware of them. What was totally forgotten becomes suddenly remembered.

I was not looking for anything in particular when I did this exercise with my teacher and because this dream-like life story came to me in a setting which felt to be in the 1700s or 1800s, I took it to be symbolic and not literal. I interpreted it as a past life experience. By 2015, however, I knew that the dreamscape, including the revelations: 'and so I die in my mother's womb' and 'you were never meant to be born' actually applied to my current life and did happen to me in my mother's womb in the months before I was born in June 1962.

Little did I know that doing a breathing exercise focussing on my tailbone would unlock a story from my life which had been completely hidden from me all my life. The first time the story was revealed to me, however, I didn't recognise it. I didn't think it applied to my current life. It was too abstract, too esoteric, to 'up in the air'.

This is the way it sometimes happens when you use esoteric forms of healing, such as breath work, to reveal the details of your past. It unlocks the story but not always in a way you easily understand. And this is one of the reasons why you need an experienced teacher to help guide you through.

An important insight to take away from this experience is in the way this part of my current life story was first revealed to me. It was revealed in the form of a past life dream. A story from the 1700s. From this experience and from subsequent dreams and alpha state meditations, I have discovered that the human psyche sometimes uses the medium of a past life setting to relate to the inquiring mind a story belonging to its current life. It is always tempting to believe past life stories as real things that did actually happen many years ago, but from experience, I have found that past life stories always disprove themselves as past life stories and instead prove themselves as a way of telling a current life story in a non-current-life setting. It's the way our mind works.

Revealing and understanding the forgotten or hidden reasons why your life has turned out the way it has not only helps you to forgive and move on from your past, it also sets you free of damaging emotions and subconscious patterns of behaviour you have not been able to control or understand. It is as if revealing and understanding your past acts as a reset button for your life. You are set free to start anew again.

How far back into your past do you have to go in order to be free?

Sometimes uncovering everything that happened to you during a period of hurt is not enough. You may also have to understand why everything happened before you feel yourself in the position of being able to forgive everything, including those who hurt you, let everything go and move on.

In the example of being abused by a parent, this means uncovering all the abuse perpetrated on you by that parent, including the bits they deny or have forgotten. It also means understanding why that parent did what they did to you, including the bits they do not fully understand themselves. The reasons why that parent did what they did will almost always include what happened to them in their own childhood, including what their parents did to them, which means you may have to go further back into the past when trying to uncover and understand everything. You may additionally need to discover what happened between the parent who abused you and their parents, your grandparents, and finally to understand why your grandparents did what they did to your parent.

So, in your journey of healing you may need to work with a trained professional whose methods will unlock the stories of three generations: you, your parents and your parents' parents, or if your abuser was not one of your parents: you, your abuser and the parents of your abuser. You will need a method of help that will be able to connect you to people you may no longer have any connection with, or who may no longer be alive. Finally, you will need a method of help that will be able to uncover forgotten, hidden, subconscious and unconscious details and reasons in the lives and actions of those three generations. And don't worry, it's all doable.

Working with my teacher, using only the method of breath, focus and sound, I was able to go this far back. I was able to connect with and understand people I was not, at the time, in connection with. This is how the process worked.

First, we did the breathing exercise, as described on pages 35-37, which revealed the general cause of all my anger in life: my mother. Then we repeated the exercise. Having discovered that my mother was the cause of my anger, my teacher now told me to hold an image of my mother in my mind's eye, in the space between and behind my two physical eyes, while again bringing breath, focus and sound to my solar plexus. The aim of this second exercise was to push me deeper into my anger with my mother until the thing that made me most angry with her came to me and sitting there, in front of my teacher, focussing my breathing on my solar plexus, making the sound "eeeee" on each of my exhalations while holding an imaginary picture of my mother in my mind's eye did exactly that. That's how it works. When you are angry with someone, the reason for that anger usually only reveals itself when you are pushed very strongly into that anger. Often times, why you are angry with someone today is rooted in a deeper, unexpressed anger towards that person from the past and you have to get to and release that deeper issue in order to fully release the anger you feel today.

The thing which had made me most angry about my mother revealed in this particular exercise was that she had sent me to a faraway school when I was young. The fourth layer of the onion. This school was a disastrous experience for me. In order for me to let go this school experience and forgive my mother for it, I needed to understand why she did it. She had always told me when we spoke face-to-face that she sent me to the school for my own benefit, as it had a good reputation and she only wanted the best for me. I was never happy with that reason. It never felt right. That was why, twenty years later, I was still looking for the true reason.

Now I did the breath, focus and sound exercise a third time with my teacher. Again, my teacher guided me to hold an image of my mother in my mind's eye. This time, however, she guided me to additionally bring my breathing into this area. I began to 'breathe' in and out through an imaginary hole in my mind's eye and simultaneously through the image of my mother I was holding there. My teacher then instructed me to ask my mother out loud why she had sent me to that school and to await her answer. My mother was not present in the room for this exercise. I was in Thailand. She was in Ireland. After a few minutes the answer came, not in the form of words being spoken to me, as there was no one present to speak them, but in the form of a sudden and very deep realisation that came into my conscious awareness from my mind's eye, where we store our spiritual consciousness, the consciousness that connects us to other people in spirit rather than through physical contact. From this connection to my mother came the answer. She sent me away to this school because she needed to send me away. She needed to send me away, because having me at a school closer to home would mean me spending more time at home and with her. By spending more time with her she would have to talk to me and by talking to me she would have to reveal more of herself to me. This is something she did not want to do, so she sent me away. This reason fitted. The core of the onion had been reached. This felt true, whereas the previous reason, of sending me away for my own good, never did. By doing this exercise with my teacher, I discovered information which had been hidden from me for many years and from a person, my mother, who was not present in the room while doing the exercise.

Something from my past was now revealed to me in a different light. Now I fully understood why my mother sent me away and because I now fully understood it, I was in a position to be able to process it, move on from it and forgive my mother for it. And I did. There was now nothing else left for me to learn or understand about that particular part of my life, whereas, before, when I couldn't let it go, or forgive my mother for it, it was because a piece of the story was still missing.

That's how it works. Find out who hurt you. Find out what they did to hurt you. Find out why they hurt you. Understand everything about it, then you are free to move on from it.

I successfully completed this process with my teacher using the simple tools of breath work, focus, sound, awareness and perseverance. It is a method of healing that works, although in parts it can be difficult to explain how it works, especially in having imaginary conversations with someone whose image you hold in your mind's eye. This is sometimes known as higher-consciousness communication and you need to work with an appropriately trained teacher to enable it to happen correctly. It is a form of communication you can use to connect with anyone in your life, past or present, dead or alive, who you are in connection with or who you are not in connection with and with whom you can have a full-blown but very silent and truthful conversation.

I first worked with my teacher to have these conversations with my mother but, using the same technique, I also went on to have similar conversations with my father and my maternal grandfather and grandmother, none of whom were alive at the time. Using similar technique and with an appropriately trained teacher or guide, you can do the same.

Summary.

My wish in sharing this experience with you is to show that there are ways of successfully understanding and healing yourself of your past other than through traditional therapies and medicines. This is not to say you should follow the alternative path I took. If traditional therapy is the way for you, then traditional therapy is the way for you, but please, do check that your therapist can go to the level of depth that may be required.

My teacher never used a label to describe the methodology of her work. I have always described it as a mixture of breathing, focus, sound and awareness. I think, however, certain other alternative health practices, such as rebirthing, shamanic sweat lodges and types of breath work, including holotropic breath work, do the same thing.

This type of energy work, however, doesn't bring a full healing. Its role is to open the wound for cleaning, by revealing important things to you which you may have forgotten, or which may have been hidden from you. Things you need to see and understand. This is important because if you have a physical pain in your body, such as chronic abdominal discomfort which is related to an underlying emotional condition, your body will not let go that pain until you see, understand and forgive the underlying emotional condition. Only when you understand the underlying emotional story and forgive it, will the chronic abdominal issue go. It is this latter aspect of healing, forgiveness, the cleaning of the wound, that completes the healing process and such forgiveness can only come from you, no one else.

The concept of bringing together breath, focus, sound and awareness into a single method of healing is easy to grasp and maybe you are tempted to try it yourself to see if it works, but as a person who has gone through this type of healing, I advise against trying it by yourself. You need to work with an experienced partner who knows where you are going when you don't and who knows how hard to push you when you think you have reached the endpoint when, in fact, you haven't.

From experience, I have found that a person who tries this type of healing work in their attempt to heal themselves of a past hurt can be too quick to forgive the person who has hurt them. They start the exercise. They quickly realise what it is related to. They see the person involved and say "Ah yeah, I know this story. It's my father (for example). He hurt me when I was young but it's over now. I've moved on. I've forgiven him for it". It is easier to bypass the memory of their hurt and the possible uncomfortable emotional reactions they may experience on revisiting that hurt and jump straight to forgiveness, than it is for them to go into the experience of their emotional hurt. It's normal. But it doesn't work. This is why you need an experienced partner in this particular type of healing work to push you into an area of your life you do not wish to visit.

The other reaction I have experienced is jumping to an answer too quickly. For example, if you try the breath-focus-sound exercise to open up anger you may feel you are storing in your chest, you may, within minutes of starting the exercise see a picture in your mind's eye of someone's face, such as your partner and so you quickly deduce "Aha, it's my partner!", whereas the origin, or cause, can be something or someone else. You think you've found the answer when, in fact, you haven't. You need to go deeper. If you don't, if you leave it at the "Aha, it's my partner" level of revelation, you will find, in time, that the anger you tried to release by doing the exercise will not have released and you will have to do the exercise again.

As I have mentioned before, your chosen method of healing doesn't have to be breath work or energy work, it can also be traditional therapy, such as family constellation therapy. An advantage of breath and energy work, however, is that it quickly and accurately accesses the subconscious, the body's cellular memory, where a sharper image of the past is stored. The conscious mind, by nature, can become confused or forgetful in recalling a past hurt, or it may, over time, draw a wrong conclusion relating to a past hurt because certain aspects of the hurt were never revealed to it in the first place. It is very rare that the conscious mind can relate an event from the past that is a 100% accurate reporting of the event. The body, however, through its cellular memory can. This is why it is beneficial to your healing process to include a form of healing that can access the subconscious and the unconscious planes of stored information within you, in your body.

Breath work or energy work also reveals the way your body stores your past emotional hurt. It does so in layers, like the layers of an onion. Breath or energy work starts at the outermost layer, the way you are today and works inwards, until the last, most innermost layer is revealed, the way you were at the time before the emotional hurt began. If, for example, you are someone who is generally angry in life, when you start to use breath work or energy work as your method of healing, the first thing it will do is make you angry. That's the way you are today. It will next reveal the effects that anger is having on you and your body. You will get agitated, frustrated and impatient. Your body will physically tense and tighten and you will have to work hard to release that physical tension and tightness. It will then stir up memories from the past. Memories of what happened and who made it happen. All the things that have led you to being angry today. The memories will keep coming, keep getting stirred up by the breath work or energy work until there are no memories left to come out, when everything has finally been revealed. And when you get to that point, you feel it. You really feel it. It's like landing on the ground at the end of a parachute jump. You can feel the physical quality of your body change from tense to calm. The calm that comes from there being no more pain. And when you get that feeling, you know you are at the end. This is the point where there is no more hurt left to uncover and when there is no more hurt left to uncover, there is no more hurt to make you tense and angry. You are free.

What this approach to healing also shows is the link between your emotional past and the condition of your physical body today. It shows you, for example, where you store all your anger in your body, by revealing the parts of you where you get tight and tense as your release your anger. This is important because most people are not aware of this link, so that when they normally experience tightness or tension in their body, they assume it to be a physical condition and not an emotionally-related condition. Emotions and bodily physical condition are treated as two separate issues, when, oftentimes, they are not. This leads to improper diagnosis and treatment. Your body contains a snapshot of every aspect of the life you have lived to this present moment in time, including the memories of everything that has happened in that life, therefore its condition has to reflect the overall condition and quality of that lived life.

This is the second advantage to using a method of healing that includes breath work or energy work. It improves the condition and wellness of your physical body by releasing the effects of past or present emotional trauma from it and which may have been having a negative impact on it, such as in the creation of weakness, tightness or coldness in certain areas of your body.

In describing the process of turning your attention inwards into your body, in order to set yourself free from adversity, I have focussed my descriptions on the release of anger and of events that can cause you to be angry. This process, however, does not apply solely to anger. The process described can be used to release any acute or chronic emotional state you may find yourself in, whether it be loneliness, sadness, fearfulness, lovelessness, regret or shame. Instead of using a person to focus on in your healing process, in the way I focused on my mother, focus on a theme instead, for instance the theme of loneliness.

It also applies to the release of any acute or chronic mental state you may find yourself in, such as in the belief that life is not fair; that no one listens to you; that you never get what you want in life or that no one loves you, and to the release and healing of any deeper, core feelings you may have about yourself, such as low self-worth, low self-esteem, lack of any real self-identity, lack of safety, lack of support, lack of self-love, lack of self-forgiveness and/or guilt. All can be released through the type of esoteric healing I have just described.

Each issue you choose to work through, whether emotional, mental or one of the deeper feelings, follows the same pattern of release and healing. It will first cause an energetic stimulation in your body, which will lead to a physical reaction, then an emotional reaction/release, followed by the revelation of the root of the issue you have chosen to work through. This process can sometimes happen very quickly and easily, other times not so quickly or easily, but the individual stages within the process of release and healing never vary.

*Further information about the effects of past or current emotional hurt on your body can be found in the Appendix section at the back of this book.

Forgiveness.

The last part in opening and cleaning the wound of a past emotional hurt, before you finally stitch it up for healing, is forgiveness. Forgiveness of the person who has caused you your hurt.

When it comes to understanding forgiveness, there are two types of forgiveness: human, or earthly forgiveness and divine, or spiritual forgiveness. One is tricky to do, the other is tricky to understand.

Human forgiveness recognises wrongdoing, then forgives it, whereas divine forgiveness doesn't recognise wrongdoing, therefore doesn't forgive, as there is nothing to forgive. The latter is absolute, or unconditional forgiveness.

For ease of understanding and in the context of the process of healing described in this book, let's focus on human forgiveness.

What has surprised me most about human forgiveness is the amount of forgiving that needs to be done in the healing process. If someone has hurt you, not only do you have to forgive that person for the hurt they caused you, but you also have to forgive them for all the additional ways they can subsequently hurt you as a result of all the ways they defend themselves after you first accuse them, or remind them, of the initial hurt they caused you.

Let's take the example of you being hurt or abused by someone you know. From my own experience of this situation, when you accuse a person who has hurt you of having hurt you, the first thing they can do is to deny or even lie about the hurt in question. This drove me mad. You know they did it. They know they did it and yet they deny it or lie about it. Sometimes your abuser lying about what they did to you causes you more hurt than the actual abuse.

Your abuser will also get angry with you for bringing up the past and reminding them of what they did. Their anger can become quite threatening, especially if they have used anger on you before and can cause not only you to become fearful, but others in your environment too. They then use this fear to control you and those others in your environment.

They may also try to discredit you in front of others by saying that you don't really know what you are talking about, that your recollection of events is wrong, or that you're simply making it all up or lying.

They may surround themselves with supporters, friends or family who will side with them and against you.

Finally, they may even get someone who was around at the time of the abuse, but who was not directly involved in the abuse, to reveal the true story of what actually happened. A star witness, as it were. This is a person you need to be careful of, as there is a big chance they have been told to lie against you because if they don't, something bad will happen to them. They have been threatened by your abuser. This can even be your mother lying to protect your father, who is the abuser, because if she doesn't, he will hurt her.

This is a difficult situation, but there is a way out. You don't allow the star witness to speak. Even if you think that, in the end, they will rush to your defence and tell the truth, the chances are most likely they will not. If you make them talk and they lie, they will hate themselves for lying and they will blame you for making them lie. They will feel so bad in themselves for their actions that they will seek forgiveness for them and they will seek that forgiveness from you. The additional burden of another person's anger towards you and their subsequent need for forgiveness from you for that anger at a time when you are already having to deal with an abuser who is putting up walls of defence against you may cause you to slip deeper into your own feelings of anger and unforgiveness. That's why the only way out is to not let them speak.

Not only will such a star witness seek forgiveness from you in order to heal themselves of their feelings of guilt, your abuser will too. Not just for abusing you and then lying about it, but for all the subsequent things they do to you, your family, your friends and even their friends in their attempts to defend themselves against the truth.

Even though you are the victim, it may end up that you have to forgive your abuser nine or ten times over. It is quite a lesson to learn.

The final forgiveness your abuser asks of you is for the original event they perpetrated upon you, but sometimes before they actually admit what they did, they ask you for your forgiveness for it in advance. Sometimes without knowing what exactly your abuser did to you, you have to forgive them for it. This is not easy. But if you do not forgive them for it in advance, they may not tell you what happened. This can be because they are too ashamed of what they did to admit it. Shame is one of the most self-destructive feelings or emotions we have. Only humiliation is worse. Shame makes people carry painful secrets with them all their lives and even take them to the grave. Some people who are so ashamed of what they have done will take their own life instead of admitting what they have done. Shame has the power to take life, but that power can be completely undone with forgiveness. Forgiveness sets shame free and when shame is set free in your abuser, they are free to tell you everything.

This is the beauty of forgiveness, it sets free the worst of pain.

So, yes, it can be difficult to forgive but in forgiveness, you set everything free. Including yourself.

Learning how to forgive.

Towards the end of the healing process, when the time is right for you to forgive the person who has hurt you, you might not be able to do so. When it comes to actually forgiving that person, you feel yourself hesitate. You cannot say the words "I forgive you". It just isn't there yet. You are still not ready to forgive. Don't worry, this is not unusual.

If you are not yet ready to forgive, here is a wonderful affirmation you can use to bring you closer to being able to forgive. When you are not yet ready to say the words "I forgive you" or even "I am nearly ready to forgive you", just say the following instead:

I am open to the idea of forgiveness.

Don't direct the words at anyone or at anything, just leave it as an open affirmation and just send it out to the universe. Repeat it every day or every second day, or however frequently you want to repeat it. Keep on repeating it until one day you feel yourself naturally replacing the words "I am open to the idea of forgiveness" with:

I am ready to forgive.

This is the universe answering your prayer and bringing the realm of forgiveness closer to you. It's a natural progression. Again, just let it play. Do not direct the affirmation to anyone or at anything. Repeat it every day or every second day or however frequently you want to repeat it until the day comes when you feel you can forgive the person who hurt you. It's like planting the concept of forgiveness in the soil and watering it every day until it grows into something real.

Why it isn't always easy to forgive.

What makes it difficult to forgive is when we judge what needs to be forgiven as important, as something that matters.

One of the liberating realisations I found when face-to-face with the presence in the 'light', and which I will write about next, is that the light, God, through non-judgement of all things, makes you realise that nothing matters. Only other human beings tell you things matter. You can harbour unforgiveness all your life towards someone who once hurt you, but at the end of your life, as you approach the presence of the light, you finally realise that the only person who is harbouring that unforgiveness is yourself. No one else is. No one else in your family is. None of your friends are and God certainly isn't either. The only person who is harbouring judgement of your abuser's actions is yourself. No one else is. The only person who is holding you back from forgiving your abuser is yourself. No one else is. This is because the only person who is judging your abuser needs forgiveness is you. God isn't. And the only reason why you don't forgive your abuser is because you judge the things that they did to you as things that matter. But the message you receive from God, from the light, when you begin to relate to it all the events from your life that you think have mattered, is that they don't.

The more we judge a hurt that happened to us as something that matters, the more importance we attach to it and the more importance we attach to it, the more difficult we make it for ourselves to forgive it. Conversely, the less important we judge something to be, the more easily we are able to forgive it, as in when we might say to someone who has caused us only a small inconvenience: "Ah forget about it, it doesn't matter". So, forgiveness itself is not difficult, it is just made so by judgement.

A non-conversation with God.

There is a moment of astonishing revelation that comes to you when you are in deep calm and deep stillness, when your mind is cleared of everything that has occupied your day and you have come into the presence of the light. It is a moment that can come to you in prayer or in meditation, when you make a sincere attempt to connect with the highest form of spiritual guidance, truth or light. It is the moment when, intuitively, you realise you are facing God.

I had one such moment in the summer of 2015, when in meditation, I was trying to make a connection to the light, which was usually in the form of a small brilliant white sun and which I usually found in my imagination to be above me, in the sky high above my head. When I would see the light in my mind's eye, I would simply focus my attention on the light and ask for a little bit of its brightness to shine down on me and into me through my crown chakra, at the top of my head. All I ever wanted to do was to let the light in. However, on that summer evening, things went wonderfully different. Instead of connecting to the light and hoping that a little bit of it would shine into me, I found myself being drawn gently up and into the light and suddenly finding myself in the light, in an unlimited blank, white space. My first feeling was that there was only me in the whiteness. There was no one else. It's the same feeling you get when you stare into the flames of a fire for a long time. You lose awareness of everything else around you. It becomes just you and the fire. The second feeling I got, which came from nowhere, was that I was facing a presence within the light. I was facing God. There was no scientific proof that it was God, just a very deep belief and sense of truth that came from beyond my mind. It made me feel happy, very happy. And it made me very curious.

Facing the light for the first time, I was strongly moved to want to start a conversation with the light. I wanted to start a conversation with God. I mean, who wouldn't?

So, I introduced myself to the light. I said hello, gave my name and waited for a hello back. But nothing came. Maybe God didn't hear me. So, I said hello again and told the light a little bit about who I was and about the life I had had here on earth. As my life hadn't always gone to plan, I told God of some of the big upsets I had had in life. I think I was hoping for a sympathetic ear, or even better, a comforting word or two that everything in my future would go much better. I was talking to God after all and if there was ever going to be a word of reassurance, it was going to be a reassuring word from God. But again, nothing. No reply. I wasn't expecting that.

Being a little bit put off by God's continuing silence, I tried a different approach to see if I could tempt God into a conversation. I confessed to some wrongdoings in my life. A few midsized 'sins'. It was a challenge to God. It was me saying: "Now then, what do you have to say about that?" and, of course, I was expecting words of forgiveness and words of understanding. I was expecting God to say: "That's OK, I understand, you tried your best, all is forgiven". But again, silence.

Now I found the silence disquieting. Was the light just not listening? Didn't God care?

But God, the light, does care and the way it cares about you is to not judge you. It doesn't forgive you for your wrongdoing, because in order to forgive you, it first must give recognition to your wrongdoing and in giving recognition to your wrongdoing, it judges you a wrongdoer. But the light doesn't do that. God doesn't do that. God doesn't judge you. Not even for the smallest of nanoseconds. It is an enormously powerful lightbulb moment. Suddenly you get it and you realise that the light doesn't judge. You can say whatever you want to God and God will not judge you.

The relief you feel. The weight that is taken from your shoulders. It is a moment of total and utter freedom. And when you are totally free, what you experience in yourself is your true state of unbounded joyfulness and happiness and love. This is the way God loves you. God sets you free. He sets you free of the one thing that blocks you from love, judgement, and of the creator of that judgement, your conscious mind.

In the presence of God, you can also ask: "Well, what about terrorism and acts of terrorism and cruelty?" and yet again, God does not reply. God will not judge. Not only does God not judge you, God does not judge other people. And when you feel the truthfulness of not judging other people, as shown by God, you suddenly self-realise that you should not judge others either.

The light also makes you realise that nothing really matters. Only other human beings tell you things matter. You can feel bad about yourself for years for having done something wrongful in your past, but in the end, in the presence of the light, you realise that the only person who is feeling bad about yourself is yourself. God isn't feeling bad about you. The only person who is harbouring judgement of your actions is yourself. God isn't judging you. And the only person who is holding you back from being forgiven is yourself. This is because the only person who is judging you as needing forgiveness is you. God certainly isn't. That's why God doesn't forgive. And the only reason why you don't forgive yourself is because you judge that the things you did, or the things that were done to you, as things that matter. But the message you receive from the light, when you relate to it all the events from your life that you think have mattered, is that they don't.

This is the way God is. God doesn't talk to you. God doesn't talk to you because to talk to you is to judge you and God doesn't judge. By not judging you, God sets you free; totally and absolutely free. Free of guilt. Free of pain. Free of memory. Free of thinking everything matters. Free of all judgement and free of the mechanism that constructs and believes in judgement: your conscious mind. God is beyond all that. God is beyond mind. This is why the only true conversation with God is actually a non-conversation with God.

It is the same as the wisdom I once received from the spirits at Wainui Falls in New Zealand:

…and is no match for the power of God
Which is beyond both recognition and unrecognition.

Forgiving everything in advance.

Although the practice of forgiving everything in advance, as outlined in forgiving an abuser for what they have done to you before they tell you what they have done to you, can initially be hard to accept and hard to do, in the end, it is the only way. It is the only way because it is God's way.

If you are in the middle of healing a period of hurt in your life, try using it as an affirmation and see what effect it has on you.

Everything is forgiven in advance

Try it in a moment of calm, in a moment of rest when you are not working on anything.

You may find that as you use this affirmation, it opens to you the next wave of pain from your hurtful past which you need to release from your body. It is as if by saying "Everything is forgiven in advance" you are setting free all the hurts you are carrying inside you, even those hurts you have yet to fully uncover and explore. And because in using the affirmation you are setting free the next wave of hurt from your body that you have yet to fully uncover and explore, you are setting it free before it grows to have a strong emotional effect on you. You are setting it free to leave your body without your judgement of what it is, who did it to you, or why. As the pain leaves your body it says "Thank you". You can actually hear the two words being whispered in your ear. Thank you for not forcing the nature of the pain to reveal itself to you and thank you for not forcing the perpetrator of that pain to reveal their own life pain which caused them to hurt you. It is a beautiful moment.

Remember, you also absorb a snapshot or 'ghost image' of the life pain of your abuser at the time they perpetrated their abuse on you, so it does happen that when releasing a painful event from your life, you may also have to release this secondary snapshot of your perpetrator's pain. By using *Everything is forgiven in advance*, this process is made much easier, resulting in you feeling less pain.

Although the effect of *Everything is forgiven in advance* is to set you free of all prior emotional pain, not everyone is ready for it. I certainly wasn't when I was still learning the lesson of forgiveness by forgiving my abuser over and over again for all the ways they defended themselves against revealing their actions. And so it may be for you too. And if it is, don't worry. *Everything is forgiven in advance* is a lesson that comes during the later stages of learning about forgiveness. If you're not there yet, you soon will be.

Of all the affirmations I have ever used, *Everything is forgiven in advance* is the most healing and the most liberating. By using it, not only does it move you to forgive someone who may have hurt you but it also works to set you free by setting you free from the process of judging whether you, or another person needs forgiveness. It is the same method of liberation through unconditional forgiveness used by the white light.

To forgive or not to forgive.

There is a balance in life: the balance between forgiveness and unforgiveness, the balance between things mattering and things not mattering. In the conscious mind, in the realm of the ego, things matter. In the unconscious mind, in the realm of the spirit, they don't. As we are physical beings in which both our ego and our spiritual selves coexist, we can access both these wisdoms at the same time and weigh them up within us. How we weigh them up depends on which of these two aspects of ourselves, our ego or our spirit, we most closely associate ourselves with. How others suggest we weigh them up similarly depends on which aspect of themselves they most closely relate to. This is why some people who more closely associate themselves with their ego will tell us not to forgive and to seek some sort of revenge or payback from our perpetrator, while others who more closely associate themselves with their spiritual side will counsel us to forgive and move on. Two contrasting pieces of advice, neither of which is ultimately wrong.

Don't forget, in the end everything is forgiven. Everything. Because, in the end, none of it matters. You will not be judged if you do not forgive. You will not be judged if you do forgive. You are given the freedom of choice to decide for yourself whether to forgive or not to forgive and that freedom is always honoured. God does not interfere with your freedom. If he did, then it wouldn't be freedom.

When the prodigal son returns home, the father doesn't ask: "What did you get up to when you were away? You did what?? You idiot!". The father is just happy to see his son again. That's the way God is with us when we return home.

The great thing, however, about the practice of human forgiveness is that the more you forgive, the less you need to forgive and the less you need to forgive, the less your need to forgive. This works to open your heart to love and as it does, the freer you become. The freer you are.

Is it possible to forgive and to forget?

From the spiritual point of view, there is nothing to forget, as there is nothing to forgive.

When you have done wrong.

You cannot change the past, but you can let it go and undo its effects in the present.

You cannot change something that has already been done, but you can undo it. You undo it by asking: Would I do the same thing now? If the answer is no, then you make the positive affirmation:

From this moment on, I would not have done that / said that / thought that.

This breaks the event into two distinct parts: past and present. Instead of keeping the event as a continuing thing in your life, linking your past with your present, by breaking the event into two halves, you are stopping the flow of energy from the past entering into your present. By doing this, you begin to let go the past event as its energy is no longer relevant, as you have now said to yourself that from this moment on, the present, you would not do what you did then, the past.

What you did then served a specific purpose in a specific set of circumstances, but as those circumstances no longer exist there is no longer any need of the event and its consequences, whether emotional or mental.

As there is no longer any need for the event, it is free to be set-free. It is free to go. You are free to let it go.

Although this is a way to help with self-forgiveness, it can also be used in helping to forgive someone else as it is often the case that if someone else once acted a hurtful event upon you, they did so as a reaction to specific events and circumstances that were particular to them in their lives at that moment in time. By understanding this, you can ask that someone else, whether through face-to-face or higher conscious communication:

Would you do now what you did then?

You can also ask:

Was it your intention to create what is now happening or what has since happened with that event?

The answer to these questions is usually "no".

With the answer "no", you can then ask:

So, what happened?

And from that question, asked without emotion or judgement and asked with the promise of *everything is forgiven in advance*, can come a full confession, a full answer, a full apology. And with that the understanding necessary to forgive and move on.

This is the process I use in my one-to-one healing work when I am massaging someone who is carrying the effects of prior hurt in their body. In my massage work, I connect with the energy of my client's hurt that is stored in their body. In that connection, I find the snapshot of the perpetrator's energy which is also still being held in my client's body. From within that snapshot, I connect to the perpetrator themselves and start a silent conversation with them, the outline of which I have just described. Working with an open heart and with a little patience, the perpetrator reveals all that happened and why. After revealing the why, they then apologise for all that happened and as soon as they say they are sorry, they let go. They let go because apologising for what they did marks the end of their process, but as they let go, so too is the energy of the hurt, from its point of origin, the perpetrator, let go in the body of my client. It's like the finger has been pulled out of the dyke. Once the origin has been let go, it frees the way for all the subsequent hurt in my client's body to be let go. I can physically feel it in my client's body. The parts of their body which had been hard and tight due to the holding on to the aspects of their hurt which had yet to be revealed quickly release, soften and become warm. For how can you still hold on to something, when that something has now been let go. Your perpetrator letting go what they did to you is as equally an important part of the healing process as you letting go what your perpetrator did to you.

At the end of the massage, I will sometimes relate the story of my silent conversation to my client. I tell those who I know already know the issue they have come seeking help for. When I tell them the story, I can see in their countenance that something shifts, something softens. I can see they have found a piece of the jigsaw that up to then had been missing and with that missing piece comes a greater understanding, a greater freedom and a greater peace.

I do not tell those in whom I find something they are clearly not expecting or looking for. There is no need to force something before its time. But I know that my client will still feel the benefit. I know they will feel something free itself up from somewhere deep inside themselves. Sometimes they may get an inkling of what it is in an afterthought or in a subsequent dream, but other times they won't. That's the way it sometimes works and I cannot control that.

Closing and stitching the wound for final healing.

1. Healing the bond between you and the person who hurt you.

Once an emotional hurt in your life has been fully revealed, understood and forgiven, it is ready to be stitched up for final healing. The way you stitch up and heal an emotional hurt in your life, such as an abusive childhood, is to first heal the bond between you and the person who hurt you, for example, a parent.

The way to do this is to first find the moment in your life before the abuse started. Then you find the moment in the life of your parent, before they had any intention of hurting you. Then, in your mind, you overlay those two moments on top of each other. This creates a moment between you and your parent when your parent didn't want to hurt you and you when weren't being hurt by your parent. A moment without hurt. By focussing on this moment in your mind with your energy, you give it strength. This heals the bond between you and your parent at *that moment in time* and creates the first healing point in healing the bond between you and your parent.

Then, again using your mind, focus on that healing point from the past and gently bring it into the present and apply it to the present. In the present moment remember there was a time when, between you and your parent, there was no hurt. This works to bring the power of a healed moment from the past into the present and creates the second healing point in the bond between you and your parent. By holding these two healing points together in your mind, the past and the present, you can join a line between them. You are, in effect, stitching them together. You are stitching up the now cleaned up wound between you and your parent. The present, it must be said, should also be a moment when there is no hurt happening between you and your parent and a moment from which you sincerely want to heal everything between you and your parent.

Finding the moment in your life before the hurt started is not always easy. Such a moment can be in your earliest childhood, in the womb or even before your conception. Sometimes you have to go very far back into the past to find the point in your life before the hurt started, but that point is there. When you find the moment of no hurt in your life, you will see that it coincides with the time in your parent's life when they had no intention of hurting you: the first healing point in the bond between you and your parent.

2. Healing your own life.

When you find the point of no hurt in your life, before the hurt started, you can create a link or a bridge between that moment in time and the present moment in time and understand that there was a time in the past, then, when everything was alright and there is a time in the present, now, from when everything can be alright. It was only in the intervening time, between then and now, that things were not alright. Once you can see this, understand it and begin to feel it, you are closing and healing the wound in your life. You can even heal a whole lifetime of hurt.

It can be difficult to see this arc of healing before you start your journey of healing or while you are in the early stages of healing, when all you are surrounded by is the pain of all the things which have gone wrong in your life, but a point comes on your journey of healing when you intuitively know that there is no more hurt left to be revealed in the process of revealing your hurt and that is the moment you begin to see the arc, the moment you can first see the start and finish lines coming together.

A simple drawing to help you visualise the arc of healing.

Here is a suggestion to help you see the arc of healing, if you are having difficulty conceiving it.

Draw a horizontal line, in pencil, on a blank A4 or some similarly sized piece of paper. About two inches in from the beginning of the line, mark a spot on the line with the letter X. This marks the time in your life when things started to go wrong. About an inch before the end of the line, mark a spot with the letter Z. This marks today. Now create a positive affirmation for today, such as 'Today is a good day. Everything is fine and everything is going well'. Something you would also have felt or believed in yourself before things in your life started to go wrong. Write your words of positive affirmation down on the paper below the Z.

About an inch to the left of the X, mark a spot with the letter Y. This marks the point in your life before things started to go wrong, when everything was still alright. Attribute the same affirmation you created for today to this point. Write the words down on the paper below the Y. The words under Y and Z must be the exact same.

Below the section of line between points X and Z, write down 'things went off-plan a little'. Now draw a new line, in the form of a shallow concave arc, joining Y with Z. This is you linking the point in your past when you were full of hope and positivity with the present, when you are again full of hope and positivity.

Now, using an eraser, erase the straight line between Y and Z, leaving only the arc joining the two points. Then erase the words 'things went off-plan a little', leaving only your positive affirmations. Leaving only hope and positive belief. All else has been erased.

By reconnecting the strength and power of the hope and positive belief you had in your past into your present, it works to unleash years of hidden inner strength and power into the affirmations of hope and positive belief you create for yourself today. You are also working to reconnect and realign yourself to your soul path and by doing so, you are laying the foundation for a smooth and straight road ahead of you.

And don't forget, not only have you now put yourself in a position to realign yourself to your soul path, you have also stitched up and healed the bond between you and your parent and stitched up and healed your own life. That's an enormous amount of work to have achieved and for that you deserve an equally enormous amount of credit.

My own healing points.

The place I found from where I could begin to put everything right again between me and my mother, from where we could start out over again, was in the time in her life just before she conceived me, at a time when she hoped everything would work out well.

This was the moment from the past that I could bring into the present, stitch the two together and in the present, say to my mother:

"I will never hold it against you for taking the decision you did (to have me). I will always respect you for what you did and why you did it. You took the only decision you could. You did the best you could do under the circumstances and, for that, I will always be thankful and grateful. Yes, things didn't work out, things didn't go according to plan, but that doesn't mean we can't start out again and have the life we both hoped for, that we can't get it right the second time round. We can".

It was a moment in our lives when no wrong had taken place between us, so it was a moment in which everything was forgiven, because there was nothing to forgive. It was a *forgiveness point.* It was the moment from which everything could start to be forgiven between us. It was the moment from which everything could be healed between us.

The fact that I was not born at this moment in time did not matter. It was only a short time before my conception, when my spiritual self, the part of me that continues on after I die, had already been prepared for my physical incarnation. I existed in spirit, but not in flesh, and because that part of me existed before I was born, it was easy to draw a line from the present moment back to then.

The first time I found this forgiveness point between me and my mother and brought it into the present, it created such a joyous feeling in me that I wanted to do it again. I wanted to bring me and my mother together again in the present moment in the energy of forgiveness. So, I did the exercise again, in the form of a semi-meditation. I imagined the two moments again: my mother full of hope just before my conception and me, with my life laid out before me, also just before my conception. I held the two moments together in my mind, with the intention of strengthening the bond of forgiveness between us at that moment in time, but, instead, and all of a sudden, I felt my mother's presence dissolve. The image I had created in my mind of the time in her life when she was full of hope began to fade. Her face also began to fade from my imagination, until all I was left with was my own moment: me just before my conception. The point in my life where I had all my life ahead of me before 'things went off-plan a little'. Then I realised. I was no longer healing the relationship between me and my mother, healing the time between us when 'things went off-plan a little', I was bringing my own healing point, me just before my conception, into the present moment and healing my own life. I was bringing my past and present together, so I could stitch both together and by doing so, heal the intervening time between. Instead of giving me and my mother the chance to start again, I was giving myself the chance to start again. I was giving myself my life back.

Everything was now free to go according to plan because the part of the journey that hadn't gone according to plan had now been rectified through the process of understanding and forgiveness. Not only had this meditation worked as a healing point, a forgiveness point, for the relationship between me and my mother, it also worked as a healing point for me and my own life.

That's how it works. Just before you are born, a life plan is put in place for you. A plan that you agree to and decide for yourself. Then, when you are born, you are born into a world where you initially have no control of circumstance and where circumstance can either conspire to keep you on your life plan, or to blow you off the course of your life plan. If you get blown off course, as I was, you have to work out what happened and sometimes you also have to work out why it happened. You could call it your life lesson. Then, when you have learnt the lesson and let it go, you are freed to start out again. You are given a second chance, as it were. You are now free to live your life in accordance with the way you originally chose it to be. The opportunity to put your life right again is always there. Always. You just have to find it and take it.

None of it is your fault.

By the time you reach the stages of finding the healing points between you and the person who has hurt you and then the healing points in your own life, you are almost home. You have done all the hard work on your journey towards self-healing. You deserve immense credit for getting so far and you should feel extremely proud of yourself for everything you have achieved.

I wrote earlier that the more deeply you go into your journey of healing, the easier it gets. The process becomes less painful, less emotional, less unending and it requires less and less mental and physical effort from you.

By the time you reach the healing points stage, you can really begin to take your foot off the gas, because what starts to happen now is that the healing process continues on inside you without you making any additional effort.

It was something that came to me many years ago in a dream that I have always called the 83–97% dream in which I received the message that spirit, or the light, comes to you when you have done 83% of your self-healing work and, from there, brings you 97% of the way home. Spirit takes over and does the last part of your self-healing for you. It is as if it is your reward for having done most of the hard work yourself.

Finding the healing points between the lives of you and your abuser, or the healing points in your own life, is symbolically bringing two points in time together, two points where no hurt is happening and then stitching those two points together as a means of healing all the hurt that had happened in the intervening time.

You create and achieve this healing with conscious effort, but what happens after you have reached this stage is something that happens without any additional effort from you.

A few months after you have done the healing points exercise, a particular realisation comes to you. It just comes to you from nowhere, from out of the blue, without you thinking about it or even asking for it. And the realisation is this. In the end you realise that although certain things happened to you, including things that may have hurt you very deeply, they actually had nothing to do with you. They didn't happen to you because of you. They didn't happen to you because of something about you. They didn't happen to you because of something you did. They were the problems of others.

Accordingly, in the final steps of your journey to self-healing, you can look back at a time of hurt in your life and you can say to yourself:

If that happened to me now
I would not think or react the way I did then.
I would realise that what was happening was not my fault and that I did nothing to cause it to happen and that no, I did not deserve it.
I was actually fully innocent at the time.
I was in a state of fully deserving the life I had chosen for myself.

Your subsequent beliefs about yourself, which stem from all the hurt that happened, begin to unravel themselves in you. You can actually, physically feel the energies of your self-beliefs untangle themselves and release themselves from inside your body. Beliefs such as:

It was my fault
or
I deserved it.

It wasn't. You didn't.

Although your feelings of self-worth may have been badly affected by the hurt that happened to you, the state of your self-worth just before the adversity occurred was pure and clear and strong.

Your true beliefs about yourself at that time were:

I am strong.
I am worthy.
I am innocent.

And as you realise that the things that happened to you had nothing to do with you, it follows that your beliefs about yourself are still:

I am strong.
I am worthy.
I am innocent.

This is who you were. This is who you still are. This is who you will always be. Everything else is the business of others and has nothing to do with you. You are still the person you were before you got hurt. The person you have always meant to have been. The person you chose for yourself to be.

This is the revelation of innocence from within. This is the self-discovery that none of what happened to you in your life was your fault. This is how the stitching up of the wound works.

It is like when you are driving your car straight through a crossroads on a green light and another car hits you from the side having not stopped at their red light.

There are four things to reflect about this scenario.

1. The direction you were going in, as you approached the crossroads, was, and therefore still is, your true direction.

2. Up to the point of the impact, you were, and therefore still are, in a state of complete innocence.

3. As soon as the impact happens, as an adult, you know that what is happening is not your fault.

4. When you untangle yourself from the accident, you can continue on in your true direction.

Children, however, especially under the age of eleven, do not have the power of reasoning to see it this way, no matter how much we want to think they do. So, when something hurtful happens to a young child, it thinks instead: 'What did I do to cause this? I have been hit therefore I have done something to deserve being hit. I must have done something wrong. It's my fault'. Sadly, this incorrect, or twisted self-belief becomes seeded in the mind and body of the child and because the child doesn't receive any help at the time to correct it, grows into subconscious, hidden or forgotten self-beliefs in adulthood. In the final part of self-healing, the stitching up of the wound works to undo any incorrectly formed beliefs about yourself and returns your beliefs about yourself to their original and true state, to innocence, to strength and to worthiness.

Telling someone who has been hurt that it was not their fault, works to correct the misbelief that it was their fault from the outside in. It is like starting to drill a tunnel under a mountain from one end. The self-realisation that comes from within that whatever happened to you had nothing to do with you is the tunnel being drilled from the other end. At one point, both drill ends meet. And when they do, the way forward is cleared.

In short, healing is the process of untangling your car (yourself) from the car that hit you (the thing that caused you to be hurt). You have to separate all the parts which are yours from those which are not yours. When you have done that, you bring your car to the body repair shop to hammer out all the dents until your car is once again smooth and pristine. You present your wound for opening and cleaning. No part of your car ever gets broken, although as a result of the crash, parts of it can get severely twisted or buckled, such as your beliefs about yourself and about life in general which were positive before the crash but have now become negative (twisted) or in the way life comes to you and through you which was once straight and easy but is now difficult, inconsistent and uneven (buckled).

An additional affirmation for letting go the past.

This is a very powerful affirmation to do when you find yourself looking back at how things once were in your hurtful past, at how you developed a personality based on those events and how you have always blamed those events for the person you have become, yet at the same time, as you are looking back on all of it, you also find that you are beginning to get tired of blaming other people for what happened and for how your life has subsequently turned out.

That's all done.
That's all gone.
I'm not that anymore.
I'm not that person anymore.

Because, in the end, you do get tired of blaming others and when you reach this stage of your self-healing, things really begin to change.

How to love yourself when you don't yet feel worthy enough to be loved.

I have learnt from the experience of helping others through adversity that at the end of the process not everybody is able, or ready to love themselves. Even after they have done all the hard work of healing themselves of their past hurt, the after-effect of that hurt can still be there and although they would now love to be able to love themselves, for whatever reason, they are not quite ready. Self-love is still a bridge that, for the moment, lies just that bit too far away.

If this is where you are on your journey of self-healing, then I have some good news. There is a wonderfully healing exercise you can do on yourself that creates enormous warmth and joy in your body, which, if you turn into a regular practice, slowly and secretly turns into self-love. It is the practice of saying 'thank you'. Not to other people. To yourself. And one of the ways you can start to say thank you to yourself is to start to say thank you to your body or a part of your body, if you are not 100% happy with all of your body.

The first time I began to say thank you to myself, it was to my lungs. In all honesty, I actually had no intention of creating any feelings of self-love when I started out with this exercise. All I wanted to do was to say thank you to my lungs for all the hard work they had done over the years in helping keep me alive. My approach to the exercise was purely practical but after a few weeks of saying thank you to my lungs, I began to notice that as I was saying thank you to them, the words 'thank you' generated feelings of warmth in my lungs. It was as if my lungs were responding to me saying thank you to them. And when I felt the warmth in my lungs, it made me happy. Saying thank you to myself not only made me feel warm, it made me feel happy. Realising how happy saying thank you to my lungs was making me, I began to say thank you to other parts of my body: my stomach, my spleen, my liver, my kidneys, my intestines, everywhere! All I was saying to each body part was 'thank you for all the hard work you have done over the years to keep me alive'. Even on a day when I wasn't feeling so happy in myself, by saying thank you to various internal organs in my body, it created happiness in me. And from that happiness came joy and from that joy came self-love. And I have to say that I was very (pleasantly) surprised by this reaction because, as a teacher and healer, I had always told everyone that the energy and emotion of love, which comes from the heart, is the most warming and healing of all our energies but as I was now discovering, the energy and emotion of 'thank you' generates equally as much, if not more, warmth and healing as love. So, if you are not quite yet ready to say 'I love you' to yourself, say 'thank you' instead.

Try it one evening in bed, just to see how it goes. Lie down. Make yourself comfortable. Give yourself a few minutes to relax and to let go some of the things in your mind. Create some time and space for yourself. Now place your hands palms down on your chest, on either side of your sternum, covering your lungs. Feel your lungs expand and contract under your hands as they inhale and exhale. No need to do any forced full breaths or yogi breaths, just your normal breathing. Now bring a little attention to your lungs. Reflect, for a moment, on the work they do for you. How they keep you alive by oxygenating your blood with their in-breaths, while, at the same time filtering out all the poisonous carbon dioxide on their out-breaths. They do this sixty seconds a minute, sixty minutes an hour, twenty-four hours a day, seven days a week, fifty-two weeks a year, non-stop. An enormous amount of work. And for most of the time of their lives, they do it thanklessly. How happy would you feel if you were to work like this for seventy or eighty years of your life without anyone ever once saying 'thank you' to you? So, lie there with your hands across your chest, imagine all the work your lungs have done to keep you alive and say 'thank you' to them. And when you say it, mean it. It only takes a second. Now do it again the next day and the next. And soon you will feel it. Soon you will notice that as you say thank you to your lungs, they respond by getting warm. And when you begin to feel that warmth, you are on your way.

There is then a further exercise you can do which creates even more warmth and self-love in you. Lie down in bed as before, only this time put an extra pillow behind your head, so you are slightly more propped up. Lie on your back with your arms by your side. Now bring your right arm over and across your chest, cupping the outside of your left shoulder joint in the palm of your right hand. To support this movement, cup your right elbow in the palm of your left hand. Lie there for a few moments, with your right arm and left forearm resting across your chest and allow your arm and shoulder muscles to relax into the position.

Now begin to say 'thank you' to your left shoulder with your right hand, while saying 'I am supporting you' to your right elbow with your left hand. Be sure that when you say 'thank you' that you send the energy of thank you to your left shoulder and that when you say 'I am supporting you' that you send the energy of support to your right elbow.

This works to create a powerful grid of warming, supporting and thankful energy across your chest. The warmth it creates then seeps into your chest and lungs spreading downwards through your torso towards your stomach and intestines. It is an incredibly self-loving and self-healing exercise.

Continue the exercise for a good fifteen to twenty minutes. Then, if you want, swap your arms around and bring your left arm across your chest to your right shoulder, cupping your left elbow in your right palm and do the exercise a second time. You may find some difference in the physical symmetry between left and right, which is nothing to worry about, but you may also notice a difference in the way the energies of support and thank you flow from one side of your body to the other. If, for example, you feel your right shoulder being more resistant to being thanked than your left, or vice versa, see if you can feel why. Maybe one side of your body has worked over the years to be your protector side. It has been the side of you you have always turned towards any source of external pain, such as an abusive partner, thus protecting your other side. Your protector side possibly feels that its strength lies in being able to take punishment and doesn't need to be thanked because it's just doing its job, or that in accepting thanks it is somehow a sign of weakness. This is important to feel, because if one side of your body is still in protector mode, that side of you will not be very open to receiving thanks and, by extension, love, so you need to concentrate a little extra on that side of your body and tell it that there is nothing wrong in being told thank you. Respect your protector side for its role and thank it for having done its job so well. In time, it will soften, realise that it is OK to be thanked and will open itself to receiving thanks, support and love.

It doesn't have to be your lungs to start with. Maybe you don't like your lungs so much. If that's the case, then find some other part of your body, or some aspect of your body that you do like and start from there. You don't have to like that part of your body cosmetically, just like it functionally. For the job it does for you. Your hands and fingers, for example, for all the work they do in helping you type on a computer keyboard eight hours a day. Or the muscles in your legs for helping you play sports every weekend. There are hundreds of examples.

The more time you spend on making parts of your body feel warm and happy by saying thank you to them, the more it makes you feel happy about yourself within yourself. But it's a subtle transformation. You don't start saying thank you to yourself on a Sunday night and wake up Monday morning the happiest person in the world! Your happiness sneaks up on you! You will be out and about one day, doing your everyday things and instead of finding yourself in your normal everyday possibly slightly grumpy mood, you feel yourself ever so slightly happier. Without you even consciously trying to be, or feel happier, you are happier. It catches you by surprise! And, as that happiness in you grows stronger and stronger, it magically turns into self-love. The bridge that was once just that bit too far away for you to cross has now been crossed.

Taking back control of your life and turning it into something good.

Another sign to look out for to show you how strongly your heart is opening and turning towards love is how it suddenly hurts you when you have a negative or hurtful thought towards someone else.

When life has been hard on you, whether at the beginning of your life or in your later years, it works so that your outlook on life becomes similarly hard. What you live in or with, forms your everyday understanding of life. It becomes easy for you to see or expect bad behaviour in others when you have been subjected to bad behaviour in others. If you have been surrounded by a family that has not been loving towards you, you grow to expect that other people outside your family will similarly be unloving towards you. Without your heart to guide you, it becomes easy to judge and criticise others. It becomes easy to be angry with others. It becomes easy to be unforgiving of others. That's simply the way it is and it is a reflection of your view of life based on your personal experience of life.

However, in what I have just written, I have very specifically used the word 'becomes' instead of 'is'. I say it *becomes* easy to judge and criticise others instead of saying it *is* easy to judge and criticise others. This is because the action of being judgemental or critical is an after-action, or a reaction to a prior emotional experience. You experience the emotion of being unloved and you then react to that emotional experience by forming the judgement that all (other) experiences in your life will be similarly unloving.

You think after you feel.

The world is good, then you get badly hurt, then the world is bad.

Of course, and here is the important part, it also works the other way around.

The world is bad, then you experience something good, then the world is good.

In the context of where this book is and where you are on your journey of self-healing, the good that you are experiencing is your heart slowly opening to love, now that you have worked through all your previous hurt. The things is, however, although your heart is now slowly opening itself to seeing the good in life, your brain is still telling you that everything is bad in life. Your brain hasn't copped onto the fact that all the bad things are over and you are now entering the good phase. It is still telling you to see and expect bad in others. It is still telling you to judge and criticise others. Yet, your heart has moved on. Your heart is now opening to love. Life is turning good. So now suddenly what happens is that you find yourself one day thinking or saying something unfairly, or unjustly scathing of someone and as you do so, it hurts your heart. You actually physically and emotionally feel it. It is like someone with a very tiny fist has just thumped you in your heart and hurt you. Your hurtful thoughts, directed at another person, are hurting you.

This is a hugely important crossover point. It is the point where you can see, if you step back from it, how for half of the population life is hard and how, for the other half, life is good.

Life is good because the good comes from within.

Maybe for you, because of some form of chronic or acute hurt you experienced, life turned unfair. But now, now that you have worked hard to help heal yourself of that hurt, you have reached the point from where life is turning good. And it is turning good from the inside; from your heart.

The first time you find that your hurtful thoughts towards another person are generating hurt in your own self is also one of the most important freedom of choice moments in your life. It is a moment when you decide between two questions: do I continue to think and say bad things about people, knowing that to do so will continue to cause me hurt, or do I start to think and say good things about people, knowing that to do so will begin to cause me good.

The decision is yours.

This is an incredibly self-empowering moment that has the potential to turn your whole life around. It is the moment when you can decide to take back control of your life and to turn it into something good, or to leave it to continue going the way it has been, with you being the victim, with you having no control. Enjoy the moment. Enjoy making the decision and, above all, give yourself enormous gratitude, respect and reward for getting yourself to this point on your journey towards healing and self-love.

What follows can only be described as *the* point of revolution and change in your life.

The final untangling: blame, expectation and jealousy.

Blame.

In order for you to reclaim everything you are, you have to stop blaming others for everything you are not.

If, as in the road accident analogy (as described on pages 74-75), you were originally in a state of belief of deservedness and abundance but then due to the impact of others on your life, it caused you to believe you were undeserving and poor, the only way you are going to reclaim your belief that you are deserving and abundant is to let go, or stop blaming the circumstances that caused you to change your mind.

It will not work if you are trying to create positive intention in yourself to achieve a new richness and abundance for yourself if at the same time there is also a part of you holding on to the blaming of someone else for you not being able to achieve that richness and abundance. The blaming of someone else, in this example, is your mind's way of getting you to hold on to the belief that you are undeserving. You have to let it go. You have to drop the bags of shopping you are carrying in order to sign the pink slip of the car you want (page 28).

In letting go of everything, which, at some point on your journey of self-healing your heart will ask of you to do, part of what you have to let go is the blaming of others for your current unfavourable circumstances. This is a real heart versus head moment. If you continue to blame others, all it does is to keep you locked into the current situation you are trying to extract yourself from. By letting go the blaming others, you set yourself free. Free to reclaim yourself and to reconnect to all the good things about yourself that have become lost in the misdirection of blame.

Blame, like expectation, works to distract you from your own greatness by shifting your focus away from you being the source of your own greatness and onto someone else who has temporarily blinded you to your belief in your own greatness and then looking to that person to give back what they took from you, although they never took it from you in the first place. You only think they did. And then you continued to think they did. So, set them free of your blaming of them. Doing so sets you free too.

And it makes for a simple yet very healing mantra:

Stop Blaming Others.

Repeat it often and every day.

When you first start using this mantra, you may find the silent voices of others inside you; your family, your ancestors and your spiritual helpers all repeating it with you. It is that important a life lesson to self-realise and learn.

Expectation.

Why you shouldn't forgive your parents for not loving you.

This starts with a memory I recently had of hitting a girl when I was twelve years old for not stopping to disrupt a game of football I was playing with my friends. I had already asked her twice to stop and to go away but she kept coming back and ruining things. The third time she did it, I hit her. Reflecting on this memory, I now asked myself, forty-five years later, why I had done that thing. The answer that came to me was that I couldn't get her to stop doing what she was doing. I had asked her to stop but she didn't so now I didn't know what to do. I ended up punishing a girl, a female, for not doing what I wanted her to do. As soon as that realisation came to me, it brought me immediately back to my mother, for I couldn't get her to stop doing what she was doing either, which in my case was not loving me when I was very young. Being unable to get her to stop, as I was less than two years old at the time, I had no idea what else to do to get her to stop, other than through (later in life) recrimination and punishment. It had taken me forty-five years to see the connection between the girl I hit, the memory of which never left me, and the need to punish my mother in an attempt to get her to stop not loving me.

What was interesting was that the renewed memory of my mother not loving me did not trigger any renewed anger or unkind judgement towards her. I have already gone through those stages of self-healing. Instead, it triggered the following, spontaneous realisation.

When we are born, we are born expecting to be loved by our mothers. We are born needing love and to be loved because, since time began, mothers have loved their children so much so that it has become a pattern of behaviour and behaviour-related expectation hot wired into the human psyche.

Yet, it leads to great confusion when you are born, expecting to be loved and you are not. And because the person who was meant to love you didn't, you are left with the questions: what have I done to cause me to be not loved, what do I now have to do to be loved and where can I find love? And deeper still, the resulting beliefs from being unloved: no one loves me, I am not worthy of love, I don't know how to love or be loved, I don't trust love and I am afraid of love.

Yet nowhere is it recorded in any book of spiritual or human truth that a mother should love her child. Nowhere. Instead, it may be better served if it were written: 'where possible, a mother, if she is able, can love her child'.

The root of all disappointment in life lies in not being loved by a parent, in not receiving love from a parent. Yet, who said we were to get that love in the first place?

Who told us we *need* love? Why are we born into a state of needing love? And, by extension, why do we have to forgive one or both of our parents for not loving us? Who said they have to love us? It is only our expectation that they have to love us. Therefore, it is expectation that is at the root of the issue because if we didn't have the expectation, there would be no confusion, pain, disappointment and resulting negative beliefs.

Forgiveness is done on the basis of judging that someone first did something wrong, in this example a parent not loving us, but who ever said that that was wrong? And if our parents have done nothing wrong, then there is no need to forgive them. It is actually wrong to forgive them (as in forgiving a parent we are also telling them they have done something wrong).

Think also how liberating it must be for a parent to not feel guilty for not loving us, especially when they either wanted to or tried to but couldn't for some deep personal reason or that they just simply weren't able to or didn't know how to (possibly because they were too young or because they were never shown how to by their own parents). Deep, painful guilt caused by (our) expectation. "Because everyone else is doing it" has never been a good answer.

So, what to do when a parent hasn't loved you?

Here is a series of four affirmations you can use to help untangle yourself from the pain of being unloved. Two are in the usual form of a positive statement but two are in the form of a question and answer: a question you ask yourself and an answer you find from inside yourself (although being told it by someone else also helps). Their aim is to empower you by taking back your power from the person you have been giving it to, the person who has not loved you. Usually, I would suggest you try these in the later stages of healing the bond between you and a parent who has hurt you, after you have moved through the stages of anger and blame. They are not so easy to do when you first start your journey of healing but you can try them and see if they help.

Question:

I expected my parent(s) to love me but they didn't. What do I do?

Answer:

You do nothing.

You just realise.

(That it was only an expectation.)

Change your expectation.

Set yourself free of expectation.

(As expectation is the problem, not your parent(s) not loving you.)

As soon as you begin to do this, you change the power dynamic in the relationship between you and your parent. No longer is it you and your parent. Now, it is only you. This is you taking back your power, instead of giving it away to the person who didn't love you. This also works to end your role as victim as when you take back control of a situation, you are no longer the victim in that situation.

What also happens when you use this affirmation is that you move the focus away from love and on to expectation. Instead of focussing your thoughts on not being loved, you focus your thoughts on expectation. This works to stop you having a negative attitude towards love and it stops you attacking yourself on the grounds of your never having been loved and of not being worthy of love. What this does to love is to set it free from attack. What it does to you, therefore, is to set you free from attacking that part of you that concerns love, your heart, and all that resides in your heart, including your own love for yourself and your love for others.

This is you setting yourself free from hurt.

Now, the affirmation: *No Expectation.*

Use this to untangle yourself from all the damaging ties, in the form of anger, hurt and blame, that bind you to the time when you were not loved.

Expectation, like blame, works to camouflage your own power and true self by shifting the balance of power away from you and on to someone else from whom you expect something to be given to you, something you actually already have, such as love. So, instead of expecting other people to give you love, you now give it to yourself, or to be more precise, you find it in yourself, for it is already there. It's just lying under the camouflage of expectation.

Now, the final two affirmations:

Question:

What do I do in order to be the source (of love) instead of being the lack (of love)?

Answer:

Belief.

It is about belief.

Believe it and you are it.

Believe you are love and you are love.

It's all about belief and believing it.

Just believe and everything falls into place.

And lastly, the self-empowering statement:

I am love.

And with this, you begin to heal yourself from being unloved without looking to the parent who unloved you.

Don't forget, being unloved doesn't stop your own love. Being unloved just means someone didn't love you. And if your first reaction to this is 'but it was my parents', then that is expectation.

Jealousy.

Jealousy, for example jealousy of another person's financial success, acts as a block to your own ability to create your own financial wealth, if financial wealth is what you are hoping for as part of the revolution and change in your life.

Remember, your attitude to the characteristics and abilities in others is merely a projection of your own attitude to those same characteristics and abilities in yourself. The things you like about other people are the things you like about yourself and the things you don't like about other people are the things you don't like about yourself. So, jealousy of someone else's financial success is a projection of your own jealousy of your own financial success. If that doesn't make sense, it soon will.

An emotion which is closely related to jealousy is anger, which is why seeing someone being financially successful can also make you angry, especially if it is someone else in your own area of expertise. So, jealousy of someone else's financial success is actually a projection of your own anger at your own financial success. Or, if you are not financially successful in your current life, anger at yourself for having been financially successful in one of your past lives. Although that life has passed, the anger and the lesson needing to be learnt from it remain.

Let's say, for example, that in a past life you were very wealthy and that being wealthy changed the way people viewed you and interacted with you. Possibly, you were seen as nothing more than a walking cash machine and the only thing people who came into contact with you wanted to do was to get a piece of your money. Being seen as merely an ATM may also have led to you developing feelings of worthlessness, in the same way some women who are only seen for their good looks develop feelings of worthlessness about themselves. So, in being surrounded by people who were only interested in you for your money, a lifestyle which slowly began to make you feel otherwise worthless, the fact that you had money began to make you feel angry. Having money made you angry. Money made you angry. In an attempt to get away from the way life was treating you and how it was making you feel about yourself, you wished you could get rid of all of your money. Or maybe you did get rid of all of your money. You wanted instead a life without money.

And now, in this lifetime, you've got it. Only it isn't making you happy either.

So, what to do?

The answer in this example lies in finding that part of you that doesn't want money and embracing it. Letting that part of you know that you understand the lesson but that when taken to the other extreme of not having money, a life without money doesn't bring happiness either. But that happiness can lie in a middle way. Combine your past life ability to make money with your current life understanding of how to properly manage money so that you can now manage money in a way which won't attract the same kind of lifestyle or feelings of worthlessness you experienced before.

This is how you untangle yourself from a current life belief about money (I can't get it) which is rooted in a past life belief about money (I don't want it).

And then finally, forgive yourself for not wanting money and for not being able to create money.

Untangling yourself from negative beliefs about yourself stemming from prior hurtful emotional experience, whether in your current lifetime or in a past lifetime comprises a double reverse action. You have to reverse the flow of thought from being a projection onto someone else to being a self-examination and then reverse the negativity in your current thinking back to its original positivity. Instead of blaming others for your life, you take back control, power and ownership of your life. Instead of thinking you cannot, believe that you can because you are the source and not the lack. When it comes to self-healing, the eventual truth, almost always, lies in the opposite to what and where you first think it is going to be. You just have to keep going until you find it and it is my hope that this book will help show you how.

Summary.

It looks easy on paper, doesn't it? Healing. How to start. Where it ends. Opening and cleaning the wound. Stitching it up. Forgiveness. Healing the bond between you and the person who hurt you. Healing your own life. Realising that none of it is your fault. Learning how to love yourself when you don't feel worthy of love. Taking back control of your life and turning it into something good. I can only write these things because I have been through them all myself. When I started my journey of self-healing, I had no concept or idea of any of this. All I had was the anger of 'Why did you do that to me?' Years of anger, but years of anger that were making me tired and as I got more and more tired, I began to wonder 'When will this ever end?' This is why I am sharing this part of my journey with you. To let you know that it does. It does end. And that the closer you get to the end of your journey into healing, the easier, lighter and brighter it becomes until the day arrives when you just feel it in you that you have no need to look back anymore. Your journey's over. It's finished. It's done. And now you're free.

The Healing Process (II).

A spiritual-intuitive approach to healing using meditation, dreams, spiritual energy and nature.

Using spiritual energy to heal yourself.

For ten years I spent my winters in Chiang Mai, northern Thailand. I initially went there to learn Thai massage, then later to spend time with my teachers and finally to teach Thai massage at one of the big schools. Looking back, however, I realise that I also spent a large part of my time in the temples there. Chiang Mai is famous for its Buddhist temples. It is said to have 365 temples, one for each day of the year. This makes Chiang Mai a strongly spiritual city. Spiritual, not religious.

One of the great things about visiting the temples in Chiang Mai is that you can visit them anytime. They are open all day long. And when you go in, they are peaceful and quiet, colourful and perfumed and filled with dozens of beautiful golden statues of the Buddha to gaze at. There are only two rules you are asked to follow: take your shoes off before entering a temple and when you sit or kneel in a temple, do not point your feet in the direction of the Buddha.

The other great thing is that when you go into any temple in Chiang Mai, it is just you and the Buddha. There is no monk celebrating a service and even if there was, it wouldn't make much difference to you, as you don't understand Thai.

So, you just sit there or kneel. On a gorgeously-coloured red carpet facing this big golden statue of the Buddha. Nothing in the way. Nothing between you and the Buddha. A pure, direct, clear, undiluted connection. All you have to do is to stare at the gold, the statue, the symbol, and make a connection. It doesn't have to be words. It doesn't have to be prayers. You just sit there, clearing your mind of the outside world and slowly making room inside yourself for the atmosphere of the temple, the energy of the temple, the energy of the Buddha to come to you. That's what golden Buddha statues do. They are symbols. They are keys. They are gateways. When you clear your mind and gaze at a golden statue of the Buddha, the experience triggers something in you. The energy you absorb from staring at the external Buddha triggers or resonates with the energy of the internal Buddha in you, your own sense of spirit. The external spiritual connects with the internal spiritual. What is without becomes within. Oneness.

It is also like you and your best friend sitting in a quiet room together. With your best friend, you can say whatever you want. You can talk about anything, tell them about your day or relate a funny experience. Same same with the Buddha. You can share with the Buddha whatever you want. Just make the connection and start a conversation. That's all you need to do. You don't need to know about his life, where he was born, where he lived, where he died, how he died, what he had for breakfast, what he had for his last supper, who his twelve best friends were etc. That's all in the past. This is the present. It's like when you meet someone in a social situation for the first time. The meeting is focussed in the present. You don't need to understand what the Buddha did to make him the Buddha, you are meeting him for the first time now, so all you are interested in is who he is today. It is a clear, straight connection.

If you can make a connection like this with the Buddha in a temple in Chiang Mai, then you can make a connection like this with Jesus, Mohammed, Abraham or whichever spiritual figure you like, in your local church, temple, mosque, synagogue or preferred place of spirit.

I am lucky where I live. Where I live there are a couple of very old and wonderful churches in the centre of town. Hundreds of years old. Walls built of stone. And in the stone of the walls there is energy. Spiritual energy. Healing energy. Magical energy. Energy you can feel. Energy you can touch. Energy that feels like it is of very high and fine vibration. All you have to do is to rest your head or your body against one of the stone walls and you feel it. It's a bit like the feeling you get when you hold a powerful healing crystal in the palm of your hand. When I go to my local church, I don't go to listen to the priests and partake in the sacraments, I go to the back of the church, take a small chair, sit down and rest against a wall. After a minute or two I feel it. The energy. It creates a tingling effect in my body, like pins and needles and the longer I stay, the more the tingling spreads throughout my body. This is the spiritual energy of the church entering my body. This is the church and the energy of the church connecting to me, communicating with me and healing me. It doesn't matter what the energy is, or whose it is. It could be the energy of a saint the church is dedicated to, an angel, Jesus, Mary or Joseph. It doesn't matter. What matters is the connection and that in the connection, in the tingling, in the energy, you can have a conversation. And if you ask the right sorts of questions, you get the right sorts of answers. Answers to everything. Absolutely everything.

In St Stephan's cathedral in Vienna, there is a side chapel called St Eligius. Inside this chapel there is a powerful energy force. You can feel it if you sit in the middle of any of the first three pews. It is like a wide beam of invisible energy that travels up from deep within the earth, through the chapel floor and upwards and outwards into the sky. If you sit in the middle of the beam, you feel it. It is a bit like standing over an air vent outside a metro station where you can feel the air coming up from the station below, only that in St Eligius it is not air you feel, but tingling.

The first time I visited the chapel was in July 2015 after being told about it by a friend. I sat in the middle of the energy beam and I asked it "What is your purpose?" The reply was: 'To help people'. It was that simple. And that's what it does. You sit in the energy, ask it for help and it helps you. In 2016, I asked the energy to help untangle the energetic mess that was in my first chakra. I knew it wasn't an easy task, but two years later, when, for the first time in my life, I felt energy in my body move freely from my navel through to the tops of my hamstrings, I knew it was working and so I offered up a little prayer to say thank you.

Then, finally, on 3 January 2020, I had the following dream.

> I am being chased by someone, a male, through and around the grounds of an apartment complex. It is tiring and fatiguing. While being chased, I enter the apartment building and run up the stairs and into an apartment on the first floor. The door is opened by a female. She has a face I recognise, an old friend who once offered me sanctuary many years before. The man chasing me approaches the apartment with the intention of getting in but she stops him with the message:
>
> "You're a sweet man but you're just not my type".
>
> At the same time, she opens the apartment door a fraction to let another female come in. It felt like someone she was expecting. Although I would not have been happy to have the chasing male be in the apartment with me, I am OK with the idea of the female, one of the doorkeeper's friends, being in the apartment with me.
>
> Now seeing that there was no way in, or that he was not going to be allowed in, the chasing male leaves and goes away.

And, on 4 January 2020, at 02:11 in the morning I woke up with the very quick but very strong message in my head: "You are your own man now".

The energetic mess that had been my first chakra for the first fifty-seven years of my life was finally healed.

This is why I go to church; to connect with the energy that can sometimes be found in churches, spiritual energy, and to use that energy to help me in my self-healing, to recharge my batteries and to keep me going.

I have also found that I can sit in a church and ask for new ideas about what to do at work to come to me. And they do. I can wake up one morning soon after with a new and clear idea for something I can include in my teaching or in my writing.

This, for me, is what spiritual energy is. It is an energy that opens your mind to new things, new ideas and new opportunities. It brings your attention to and helps you resolve issues in your life, both past and present, which the conscious mind is unable to. You can use it to discover your true vocation in life, your soul purpose. It helps you break free of strongly-held damaging human beliefs and behaviours, such as the belief in superiority, which leads a person to believe they have the right to own and control another person, or worse, the right to use, abuse or even destroy another person; the practice of dumping your emotional baggage onto another person and expecting them to carry it for you and the hereditary behaviour of I can/will do it to you because my parents did it to me.

Spiritual energy is also an energy you can use to give yourself the strength of will and determination to get you through difficult periods in your life and, of course, you can use it to bring you feelings of inner peace and calm, of freedom and of love. For many of us who are in pain, the only place we can find where there is no pain is in a spiritual place, whether in prayer or in meditation. It is a place where we can 'be' without the judgement of others. For some of us, we find spiritual energy to be above us, as in when we seek it out through prayer. For some of us, we find spiritual energy to be inside us, as in when accessing it during meditation. While, for some of us, we find spiritual energy to be all around us, as in when we find it out in nature. It is, of course, all three. Spiritual energy is above us, inside us and around us all at the same time and all the time it is here to help us and to do us good.

The connection between churches and nature.

What is interesting about churches and the energy that can be found in them is whether the energy was there before the church was built and the church was then knowingly built over the source of energy as a means of housing it, or, if the energy in the church was created through years of devotion. I say this because the key is the energy and not the building, not the church, because if you don't have access to a church to help you in your healing, it doesn't matter. The same energy is available in nature. You can find the same connection and healing in nature as you can find in a church.

Using your dreams to heal yourself.

On 13 April 2016, I had the following dream.

> I am standing in the middle of O'Connell Street, the main street in Dublin, Ireland. People are going into the shops all along the street, taking whatever they want and then leaving. I am the only person not doing it. I am standing in the middle of the street, frozen, not moving, or unable to move.
>
> It wasn't that it was illegal to go into a shop and take what you wanted that stopped me. It was perfectly allowed. You just went into a shop, took what you

> wanted and left. You didn't have to pay for anything.
>
> From within the dream, I had to waken myself out of the dream into a half-awake state and then semi-consciously go back into the dream and force myself to go into a shop and start taking whatever I wanted, telling myself that it was OK to do so. Then, and although I was now aware that it was perfectly OK to take whatever I wanted from any shop, I still did not go into one particular shop. The LVMH shop. The luxury brand shop. I still wouldn't, or couldn't go into the luxury shop. I asked myself in the dream: why? The answer, the feeling I got was: I don't deserve it. I am not worthy enough to go into that shop.

The first part of this spiritual-intuitive approach to healing is a dream. A dream is your subconscious mind's way of telling you what you need to work on and what needs healing in order for you to live a fulfilled and happy life. This is why you should, at all times, note and journal your dreams. Only you know what you need in life and only you know what you need to do in order to get what you want or need in life. No one else does. With the information from your dreams, you now go to a church. Sit in the church, against a wall if you so wish.

In your dreams, the information you receive about your life comes from either your subconscious or your unconscious. Information about your past, including what still needs addressing in your life, is stored in your subconscious, whereas information about your future, what is about to happen to you next, is stored in your unconscious. In church, the energy of the church connects to your subconscious and your unconscious and communicates with you through both. Your dreams and the energy in the church use the same method of communication with you. They understand each other. They read each other. The energy present in your local church understands what you see in your dreams and just like the energy in the St Eligius chapel, in Vienna, the energy present in your local church is there to help you. So next time you have a dream in which, for example, you get an inkling that there is something or someone blocking you from doing or getting what you want in life, go to your local church, sit down and talk quietly to the energy that is present in the church. Just say: "I had a dream last night in which this happened (recount the whole story). I feel it has something to do with my lack of self-worth (for example). Please help me to heal this lack of self-worth and help me grow a new sense of self-worth". See if you get an answer. If not, don't worry. It may come to you in your next dream or two. If not then, it will come later in some other form. But do not doubt, for a single instant, that it will come. Once you ask, you will receive.

Almost one year to the day after my O'Connell Street dream, I was giving a massage to a client who just happened to be a channelled-automatic writer. She was able to tune into a stream of messages and wisdoms which were being transmitted from a spiritual source, such as a deceased loved one, a guardian angel or one of the higher angels, to a particular individual being here on earth. After our session ended, she said she was being asked to give me a message and she asked if I was happy to receive it. I said yes. The theme was self-worth. To help me overcome my low self-worth, it was suggested to me that, in my mind's eye, using my imagination, I build a golden room in the centre of my heart chakra, the area surrounding my heart, and fill the room every day with something gold, whether a gold coin, a gold ring, a gold ornament or a gold painting, etc. Gold symbolises abundance and by consciously placing symbols of abundance in my heart, I would, in time, feel that abundance in me, which would grow my self-worth.

There is, of course, no scientific methodology to prove the outcomes of such positive affirmations or visualisations. The only proof you have comes in those unguarded moments after you start using positive affirmations or visualisations to rebuild your self-worth, when you suddenly discover that your thoughts and your beliefs about yourself are not as negative or as empty as they once were. It is normal to expect that the use of positive affirmations or visualisations will make you feel tangibly more positive about yourself, and oftentimes they do, but what can also happen is that their use can make you feel less negative about yourself and this isn't always as easy to notice. Growing to be less negative about yourself is also a sign of growing self-worth and self-love.

Using the energy in nature to heal yourself.

In the early 2000s I lived for a short while in New Zealand. Whilst there I spent large amounts of time in nature. I was specifically searching out areas where people had described there being a strong presence of energy. I had done some research on the subject, read a few books and spoken with some highly knowledgeable locals about it. From all the information I gathered, I drew up a list of places I wanted to visit in order to experience the energy that was said to be present at each one and then spent seven months visiting and experiencing them. Because each place

I visited ended up being in the middle of nature, often in remote areas, there was never anyone else around when I got there and being on my own, I was able to do whatever I wanted. So, I began to talk to nature; to the trees, the fields, the rivers, the lakes and the waterfalls. You can do that sort of thing when you are on your own and there is no one around to judge your actions. I would introduce myself to the nature that was present wherever I visited. I would say who I was, where I came from and why I was there in that particular part of New Zealand and after a while, nature would talk back. If I was in a forest, for example, and talking to a tree, the tree would explain its role within the forest, what roles other trees had in the forest and which tree I would need to go to in order to get the answers to the questions I had. As soon as I cleared my conscious mind of all its concepts of how and with whom normal communication should function, everything became very simple. I would sit down, clear my mind, listen to the nature around me and write down in my notebook what I 'heard'.

For example, from the energy present in the fields at Te Miringa Te Kakara, in North Island of New Zealand, I was told:

The eyes do not direct the mind to interpret what it is we are seeing rather
the mind directs the eyes to see what is necessary for us to see at that moment in time.

And from a conversation I had with the trees at Wainui Falls in Abel Tasman National Park in South Island, I was told:

1.
Taking power away from others
No matter in what symbolic form
(house, land, possessions, money, children)

Does not give you power,
Does not make you powerful.
Instead it creates fear.
Fear of you in the eyes of others.
This is not true power
It is false power
(A means without an end).
The 'power' of fear
Is determined by the recognition you give it.
If you recognise, or acknowledge fear
You give it the power to be.
If you do not recognise it
Then it has no means of being
And so is powerless.
This is why power,
Acquired through the creation of fear
Is unstable
And is no match for the power of God
Which is beyond both recognition and unrecognition.

2.
In nature, the answers are there all the time.
Spirit doesn't answer each question each time it is asked.
All questions are answered all the time.
All you have to do is to have ears.
This is a different approach to teaching.

Nature is full of very powerful, healing energy. The further you can get into nature and away from the interference of man, the cleaner, purer and stronger it is and it can be part of your healing process, if you allow it. Its energy contains everything you need to know about life because it, nature, has been here since life began. It will answer any question you have about anything and it will offer you guidance towards doing the things that are good for you and living the life that is right for you.

For me, being in nature is about understanding the way life used to be, before everything got so complicated. It is an energy I use on myself and on my massage clients to help return them to the way they were before things started to go wrong for them, to just before the car crash at the crossroads. It is the energy I use to help me find my way home.

Summary.

That's how this method of spiritual-intuitive healing works. First, a dream, then asking the energy present in your local church or in nature for help in resolving the issue revealed in the dream and finally, unexpectedly, finding someone who has the answer and then putting that answer into practice. Synchronicity. Everything happening in the right order and at the right time. But synchronicity can take time. You don't ask for a healing of your unworthiness on Sunday night and expect to get it on Monday morning. The spiritual-intuitive healing process is more subtle, more esoteric, than working face-to-face with a trained therapist or health professional. The process takes time. It can take a few weeks, a few months, or even a few years. But *never does the process not deliver*. Once you put it out there, once you start asking for it, it starts to happen and it will continue happening until the end, until you receive what you ask for. And it will always bring you exactly what is right for you at the time that is right for that thing to be brought to you. It is never, ever wrong.

You are free, as always, to choose whether to believe in or not believe in this type of healing but I hope that in sharing my own experience of spiritual-intuitive healing with you, you will see that it exists and that it works.

Part Two.

Realignment.

Aligning or realigning yourself to the life you have always wanted.

No matter how hard you ask, believe and receive
if what you are doing is not meant to be what you are doing
you will struggle.

What you are meant to be doing in life is not necessarily what you have ended up doing in life. What you are meant to be doing in life is living the life you have chosen for yourself to live, whereas the life you have ended up living maybe one that has been shaped by previously uncontrollable circumstance or by the deeds and decisions of others. This part of the book is about extricating yourself from that particular life and getting yourself back to the life that you have always wanted for yourself; the one you chose for yourself to have. Your destiny.

Your destiny.

Your destiny is the life you have already chosen for yourself to have before incarnating here on earth. It is useful to know what it is, because the greatest single cause of modern day stress arises out of the difference between the life you chose for yourself to have and the life you have ended up living. Maybe your current life and your destiny life have fallen out of alignment. As a result, there will be some degree of conflict, resistance or blockage in the way life flows to you, through you and from you. Think of it as two water pipes which are at first joined together head to toe but when laid in the earth become separated and fall out of alignment. The through-flow of water is no longer what it was designed to be. This is the same as the energy of life flowing through you when you have fallen out of alignment. Things are still flowing, but not as strongly nor as easily as they should. You're having to work harder for things which seem to come more easily to others. Just willing them to flow better, while not understanding why they aren't flowing better, is simply not enough.

So, an important part of healing and getting your life back on track is to discover exactly what track your life needs to be put back on. Knowing it will, at least, point you in the direction you should be going, the direction that will cause you the least amount of future stress and the greatest amount of reward.

The details of your destiny are to be found in your spiritual self, the spiritual consciousness you bring with you into this world. This consciousness is to be found in an area of your body known as your third eye or your sixth chakra. So, one of the ways to discover the details of your destiny is to access the information relating to it stored in your sixth chakra. You can do this by following a course in spiritual development, such as meditation or by working one-to-one with someone trained in the spiritual arts. I chose the latter. Just ask the person you choose to work with to help you discover the nature of your true self, your true identity. It is not difficult to do. All it took me was the use of breath and awareness and my teacher guiding me to ask the right questions.

Alternatively, you can visit somewhere where you feel a strong connection to nature, to energy or to spirit, as outlined in the last section of this book on the spiritual-intuitive approach to healing. Go there and meditate on the theme of destiny and ask if you can be helped to understand what your destiny path is. If you don't have such a place to visit, you can always ask at home. Offer up a little prayer at night, before you go to bed, to whoever you feel would be able to help you and ask them about your destiny. And don't forget, the answer might come to you in the form of a dream, so take note of the dreams you have after you have asked for help.

While in the womb, one of our developmental tasks is to integrate our spiritual consciousness into the body we are being born into. This includes the integration of our chosen destiny. Of course, when we are born, the first thing we say to Mama and Papa is not: "Where is my application to NASA? Don't you know I'm going to be an astronaut when I grow up?", but a very vague sense of it is there. It comes out early in some people because it is needed to come out early, such as in children who grow up to become athletes or sports stars. Their success in life needs to coincide with their body being in peak physical condition, which comes sooner rather than later in life. In others, success comes later in life, such as in children who grow up to become healers or life coaches. Their destiny requires them to first accumulate life and healing experience which they can then use to create success in later life.

In the meantime, sitting between any child and its destiny, is education. Our educational system is designed to knock any sense of destiny out of us and to prepare us for a life that only other people want us to have, but that we ourselves have not chosen for ourselves to have. Sadly, due to the pressure of the system, many of us lose sight of our destiny. Our dreams get quashed. Quashed, but not extinguished!

You are free, as always, to choose whether or not to believe in destiny. The belief in destiny is arbitrary. Some people have it, others don't. There's no point arguing with non-believers that it exists, just as there is no use arguing with believers that it doesn't. I would, however, like to share with you three stories, three separate instances, where I have come face-to-face with destiny in my work. Not just my destiny, but the destinies of other people.

Three stories of destiny.

One.

In early 2015, I was giving a massage to one of my regular clients. She was thirty weeks pregnant at the time and was experiencing tightness in the tops of her shoulders, in the back of her neck and at the back of her head.

As I work on the floor, I laid my client on the ground on her left-hand side and began to work on loosening the top of her right shoulder, only to find that my intuition was calling me to investigate further down her spine. Sure enough, in her mid-back, between T10 and T9 there was a small area of acute tightness, about the size of my thumb nail.

After a minute or two of massaging the tightness, I felt the presence of anger. Not my anger or the anger of my client, but the anger of her unborn child.

As a massage therapist – and as someone who had been living partially out of their body all their life – I had become very sensitive to the energy of other people and could easily connect to the emotional energy, or emotional state of a client, often being able to read the dominant emotion they are feeling at the time and also the underlying event that is causing them their emotional state.

In this particular massage, I connected to the anger of my client's unborn child and quickly found the reason for their anger. Her unborn child was angry with her father because, in her eyes, he wasn't taking her impending birth seriously enough. I felt the words 'he needs to focus', 'he needs to concentrate' and 'he needs to take things seriously' come strongly into my awareness.

I had connected with the spiritual consciousness of the child and although still unborn, the child had absolute knowledge of their direction and purpose in life. It was clear that this unborn child wanted to be an intellectual, academic type and a medium-to-high achiever. Although I had my eyes closed for the duration of the massage, I could clearly see, in my mind's eye, the outline of a blue tunnel with ghostly white faces of people from the past placed at intervals along the tunnel walls. I immediately understood that the tunnel represented the soul consciousness of the unborn child, its path, its journey, its destiny, extending from the past to today through many lifetimes.

I spoke with the unborn. I asked her "what about love?" and "what about fun and play and support and the bonding necessary for a healthy start in life?" It felt to me as if the spiritual consciousness of the unborn hadn't yet fully integrated itself with its human consciousness and that I was using words like bonding and support with her that she simply had yet to understand, although she clearly already knew her life purpose, her destiny.

Then, two and a half years later, in September 2017, I was again massaging this particular client. Her daughter had been born and was now two years old and the bond between her and her mother, my client, was very strong.

In the middle of my massage, I suddenly, once again, felt the presence of the daughter. This time she was happy. Very happy. She was very happy with her mother and everything her mother had done for her and she wanted me to pass this message on to her. She also asked me to tell her mother that her future was going to lie in the practice of law and that she wanted to be taken to a particular courthouse where she could absorb the energies of the procedure and practice of law from the building. When I related this to my client, she was in a state of disbelief. Without my knowing anything about my client's ancestry, she told me that her grandfather had been a judge and that she knew the exact courthouse I had just described. Surprisingly, however, it was not to be my client, the mother, who was to take her daughter to see the courthouse. This was to be the role of her father, a role she needed him to take seriously, so he could help her fulfil her destiny.

Two.

Around the same time, I visited a good friend in Slovenia who was fourteen weeks pregnant. During one of our conversations, she told me of a very abstract dream she had recently had of aliens and metal objects, which had the shape of fasteners or clasps.

The dream, although highly abstract, was her mind's way of interpreting the process that was going on in inside her womb of the human consciousness of her unborn daughter, as symbolised by the metal clasps, trying to grab onto and hold her spiritual consciousness, as symbolised by the alien life-form*. The integration of her child's destiny into the circumstances within which it is going to be born.

Fantastical dreams like this are unusual. Not every pregnant woman has them. My friend had been doing yoga and spiritual self-development work for many years, so her levels of conscious awareness had become a little more heightened than usual and when your conscious awareness is heightened like this, you sometimes see things in a way that is different to the way most other people see things.

*Anytime you dream of someone you know but who in the dream appears to you in some sort of alien form, it is just that person coming to visit you in your dreams in their spiritual form. Our conscious mind, when it is touched by something that comes from outside its own realm, the physical world, interprets that something as alien to it and so labels it as such: alien, often giving it an alien-like appearance. Dreaming of aliens is not always dreaming of aliens from another planet, it can sometimes be dreaming of someone you know who just happens to be coming to say hello to you in your dreams in their spiritual form.

Three.

My own destiny as revealed to me in a dream I had in which I saw myself in the following setting:

> A short while before I was conceived, I was standing in a large, narrow courtyard, filled with hundreds of people. It felt like a planning centre, or a task-setting centre for people of varying professions, including

journalism. It certainly felt as if I was a journalist there and I was waiting for my next assignment.

There were also a lot of people testing their footballing skills by chipping a ball onto and along an elevated pathway. The better your kick and the more the ball travelled along the pathway, the better a footballer you were. It became my turn to kick. I missed the elevated pathway completely. I looked down and noted I was wearing the wrong shoes for chipping a ball into the air.

Then I found myself standing at a table on which published news stories were pinned. There were about nine or ten stories. I guessed that the one you chose would be the one you would further report on. I was strongly attracted to the news story at the very top left. It was set in Kiev, Ukraine. I knew instinctively that the story was wrong; that the journalist had made the whole thing up without actually talking to anyone involved, doing any research or getting any facts to back their story up. Immediately I said I wanted to write that story, to re-write that story, to correct that story and to write a factual, truthful account and not just something made up in my imagination. I knew it would be a difficult task as I didn't speak any Russian and, in order to write the story, I had to go to Kiev, Ukraine.

I was fifty-two years and one day old when I had this dream, on 20 June, 2014.

Thanks to the work I had done with my teacher over the years in Chiang Mai, I had grown able to interpret some of the symbols in this dream. 'The very top left' refers to the very top left of a person's energy body, the left side of your sixth chakra, where your spiritual wisdom and insight reside. The destiny I chose for myself in this life was to rewrite, or correct, spiritual writings.

What this dream about destiny also shows is that not everyone is destined to be a footballer in life. Some people are destined to be a journalist instead. Some people choose an easy task to perform, others a more difficult one.

This is important to know, especially if you have chosen a challenging path for yourself, as it corrects the popular judgement held by some people that the proof of finding your way and of being on the right path is directly proportional to the ease with which you live your life or is directly proportional to the amount of popular recognition and reward you receive in life.

Yes, you can go on to become the successful footballer you chose to be, yet suck at being a parent because you spend so much time away from your family, playing football. As a successful footballer, you receive reward and recognition from hundreds of thousands of people.

Similarly, you can go on to become the successful parent you chose for yourself to be, yet suck at playing football, because you spend so much time away from football, being with your family. As a successful parent, you receive reward and recognition from only a small handful of people.

Who is the more successful?

Do not let others judge how successfully you are living your life on the basis of popularity and reward. They do not understand what they are talking about. Just because what you have chosen to do is challenging and does not bring you a lot of real-world reward, it does not mean you are not on the right path. Only you know that.

The same applies to manifestation. It is easy to use the measure of real-world reward as the proof of successful manifestation, yet in your efforts to manifest a successful life for yourself, you may be moved to manifest what is right for you, your destiny path, and this may not result in the real-world reward you hope for. Success can be in finding what is right for you and not necessarily in earning $100,000pa. Be aware.

Although the three stories I have just shared appear on the surface to be very different and unconnected situations: a massage with a client, a conversation with a friend and a dream I had, they are three ways of relating the same thing: destiny. My personal experience of destiny has now been too strong for me to ignore. I do believe we choose a general direction for our lives to go in. I also believe that for many of us, we lose sight of this, but what I also and finally believe is that we can, at any time in our lives, discover or rediscover what that life choice is and then, from that moment of discovery onwards, begin to live our lives in accordance with the life we chose for ourselves, the life that is right for us.

People to help guide you towards the life that is right for you.

Your spiritual family.

Although you may be part of a large family of parents, grandparents, uncles, aunties, brothers, sisters, children, nephews, nieces etc., within your family you also have a special, inner circle family:

your spiritual family. Your spiritual family are just that. They are the members of your family who also help you out spiritually. They will come to you in your dreams throughout your life to remind you of things you have to do, any life lessons you have yet to learn and to tell you whether or not you are on the right path. Sometimes you dream of them in different roles. For example, one of your spiritual family members might be your mother, yet in your dreams sometimes your mother doesn't appear to you as your mother, she can appear to you as your wife or as your sister. It can be a little unsettling if you ever dream of your mother as your sister, but don't worry, the interchangeability of your mother in her roles in your dreams is simply your mother showing you that she is part of your spiritual family as well as your earthly family.

It is not necessary in life to know who your spiritual family are but it can be very helpful, as they are the members of your earthly family you can talk to at night in your mind if you ever find yourself in a dark place and you need someone to help you or comfort you. The effect of talking to them is to raise your spirits and to give you the strength to keep going. They can also come to you in your dreams to show you the way through any predicament you may be experiencing but you would need to learn the way they share this information with you, as they won't just tell you 'do this' or 'do that'. Instead, they might bring you a picture or an object which has a hidden meaning for you or show you a very abstract movie. They don't bring you the answer, they bring you the key that unlocks the answer. If you then reflect or meditate on the key, the answer it holds is unlocked. You get the answer to the way through. An answer that always, in the end, comes from deep within your own self.

Interpreting dreams can be tricky. I wouldn't suggest you start out doing it by yourself, as sometimes a symbol in a dream can have different meanings and you could choose the wrong one. For instance, you could see your grandfather in a dream and so believe the dream to be relating to your grandfather, yet the symbol of your grandfather may also be a symbol for your own internal male side, so the dream is actually about you looking at the male side of yourself. Seek help first. Ask someone trained in dream interpretation, especially someone trained in the energy-spiritual arts, such as a shaman. Start by journaling your dreams. Write them down. If you start to journal your dreams, even if you rarely dream, you will find that you will begin to get more of them and they will grow in importance and relevance. If your spiritual family see you paying attention to them when they come to you in your dreams, they will come more often and bring you more important information.

I never knew anything about spiritual families until I was forty-two, when one day in March 2005, with my teacher in Chiang Mai, we did an unusual meditation in which I concentrated on the colour red and, using my imagination, focussed the colour red into the centre of my head, behind my eyes. When I felt I had the colour red fixed in the centre of my head, my teacher instructed me to ask out loud the following questions: "Who is dependent on me?" and "Who am I dependent on?". The following answers came:

Question 1: Who is dependent on me?

Answer: Mother, father, grandad [my grandfather on my mother' side].

Question 2: Who am I dependent on?

Answer: Love your grandad and he will look after you. Let your nana [my mother's mother] look after you.

Then a message came from my father: 'Don't forget about me. I am taking responsibility for you. I am your teacher'.

In the years following this meditation, I have received enormous support from both my grandad and my nana in my dreams. My grandad appears in my dreams to give me strength and my nana appears to give me direction. She is the one who always tells me if I am on the right path or not. The way she communicates this to me in my dreams is very simple. When everything is going according to plan, she smiles and when it isn't, she doesn't.

Although it took a meditation I did with my teacher when I was forty-two to remind me that my nana was part of my spiritual family, I think I had always had the feeling she was someone special in my life, even though she died when I was eight. And it is something I have subsequently found in my experience of helping others in my massage-healing work.

There is usually someone who was very special to you when you were young. A grandma, a grandad, a grand-uncle or even a family friend. Usually someone outside your immediate family. Someone you always loved being with. Someone you felt safe with. Someone who never hurt you. Someone who always encouraged and supported you. Someone who always loved you. A kind of a guardian angel, or if you take away the words 'a kind of': a guardian angel.

I have found from experience that it can be of real benefit to us in adulthood, when we are going through a difficult period, to look back on our childhood to see if there was anyone who fulfilled that role in our life. It doesn't matter if that person was only alive for a very short period of your life. If they were a guardian angel to you then, they will still be a guardian angel to you now.

If you do remember such a person in your life, say a little prayer to them one night. Reconnect to them. Re-establish your bond with them. Tell them all that has happened since you last saw them and where you are in your life today. Chances are, they already know and because they can see you from 'above', they can also see exactly where you are within the bigger picture of things. It is like they are able to look down on where you are in the maze and see where all the paths lead, whereas for you, being in the maze, all you can see are the walls surrounding you. So, talk to them and if you happen to be feeling a little lost in life at the moment, ask them for help and guidance. They will know the way out. That's their purpose: to help you. They are a part of your spiritual family. They are a part of your life. They are a part of you.

Creating and keeping images or memories of your spiritual family in your head is a good place to keep them, but it is not always the best place for you to keep them. When you get used to the idea of your spiritual family and you know who they are, instead of imagining them in your head and praying to them as if they are 'up there' looking down on you, try imagining them in your heart. Try to imagine them in the centre of your sternum, close to your heart. Fill your heart with them. As they are here to bring you love, you will be filling your heart with love. And the stronger you place them in your heart, the stronger the feeling of their love for you grows.

If you have been badly hurt in life and your heart is empty of love, one of the ways to start filling it is to fill it with the love from your spiritual family. Love, in its spiritual form, is unlimited and unconditional.

Spiritual friends.

You can also be visited in your dreams by people you have been kind to, for example a friend you once helped through a difficult time. These are lovely dreams. These people are your spiritual friends, real-world friends from the past or present who help you out spiritually. They come to you in your dreams to say thank you for helping them out and to bring you a symbolic gift of their thanks, such as a ball of very bright white light. They can also come to say "I love you" by bringing you a token of their love, such as a bunch of beautiful flowers, or they can come to bring you a healing to a part of your body that needs healing. Sometimes they will speak to you. They might say "this is my gift to you, thank you". Other times they might simply smile. Dreams like this are here to remind you that all the good things you do for your fellow beings are noted and rewarded. You may not get real-world rewards, such as money or recognition for your good deeds, but you get rewarded in spirit.

Spiritual helpers.

Not only do you receive help in your dreams from your spiritual family and friends, but you can also receive help in your dreams from other people, both dead or alive, who are well-known as healers or helpers.

I had one such dream in August 2016 which I would like to share as a means of a simple explanation of what these dreams can feel like. These are the notes I journaled on awakening after the dream.

> I am in a building which I know to be special. There is a bed in one of the bedrooms on which I want to sleep but I know it is not my bed, so if I do get to sleep on it, I will be stealing a sleep on it.
>
> Somehow, I do get to take a sleep on it. However,

I am soon disturbed and awoken by a room full of people, swirling around each other and dancing around the room.

[The scene ends].

Later I wake up, still on the bed, but with two figures very close to me. In a moment, I see their faces and recognise who they are.

Behind my left shoulder is a woman very closely resembling Louise Hay* that I guess it to be her. To my right, standing at my ribcage, is BKS Iyengar**. Initially my breathing freezes. I am unable to breathe as in other dreams I have had in which I have had visitations, but BKS Iyengar turns to me and says it is OK to breathe. So, I begin to breathe normally.

Louise and BKS are working on my energy body. It feels like they are heating it. I feel my body getting physically warmer. I am so surprised and happy to see Mr. Iyengar working on me that I direct most of my conversation towards him. I ask him why is he here, helping me but it is Louise who answers: "Jesus has appointed you the special son of BKS Iyengar".

I have my right arm around BKS Iyengar's waist. I feel a 'plastic bag' in his body, under the right side of his ribcage. I ask him "How are you?" and he replies "Not so well", but this doesn't stop him from smiling and from doing his work in healing my energy deep inside the lower right side of my own ribcage.

I have never met Louise Hay or BKS Iyengar. I have no connection to either, yet, they came to me in my dream to help me out. And I am no one special. So, if they can come to me in my dreams to help me out, then they can come to you in your dreams too. They possibly already do. Even if you are not aware of people helping you out in spirit, they are.

* Louise Hay (1926–2017) was the author of several best-selling self-growth books including *You Can Heal Your Life* and *Heal Your Body*. She founded Hay House Publishing in 1984.

** BKS Iyengar (1918–2014) was the founder of the style of yoga that came to be known as Iyengar Yoga and was considered one of the foremost yoga teachers in the world.

I love the spiritual family. When I have worked with people who have been surrounded by a lot of hurt in their lives, I always ask: "Was there ever someone in your life you could go to and feel safe with. Was there ever someone you loved being with?" I suggest that such a person might be their guardian angel and that if they start to say hello to them again, maybe at night before they go to sleep, that their guardian angel will come to them in their dreams to comfort them, guide them, strengthen them and help them out.

I also talk about the spiritual family to people who have been living an everyday life all their life but who are now getting a growing sense that they are being called to do something else, for example to follow a spiritual path in their lives.

From experience, I have found that one of the reasons why adults are reluctant to start a spiritual way of life, especially in their midlife years and even if it is their chosen destiny to do so, is because they think it will be a lonely way of life. Well, that's both true and not true. If you have been living a socially-accepted lifestyle all your life and you suddenly announce to everyone that you want to walk away from it so you can go on a journey of personal spiritual exploration, you may find that some of your friends won't understand. It's a normal reaction, but if you are to follow what is inside you, it might be time to let go those people who no longer understand you or what you want to do. You are changing from the old you into the new you and as you do, your environment and the people in it will similarly change. It is like you are changing from a caterpillar into a butterfly. You no longer need to eat leaves, because from now on, you will be eating nectar. You no longer need to stay in the one place, on the one leaf, on the one branch and on the one tree. You can go wherever you want and you will need to go wherever you want because you will find that trying to get nutrition from one leaf, one branch or one tree might no longer be enough to sustain you.

Your friends, the people who feed you, support you, nurture you and understand you may no longer be from the place they were before. They may be scattered. In different cities, in different countries. This is the new way. You may not see them every day because they are so scattered, but when you do see them, they will nourish you sufficiently to cover the days you do not see them. Alternatively, you can move from where you are to where they are, so you can grow more quickly into your new self. And in the intervening times, you have your spiritual family to look after you. Your angels, your guardians, the family members who have always loved you and all the other friends and helpers you will meet in your dreams and meditations. Friends who are always there for you. Friends you can talk to at any time. Friends who understand you. Friends who can guide you in the way that is appropriate for you. The new kind of leaf. The nectar. But this doesn't mean you can't return to the tree where you grew up. There will still be nectar for you in that tree's blossom too.

Astrology.

As well as choosing your spiritual family and spiritual friends to help guide you towards and along your destiny path, you also time your birth in accordance with the various astrological systems of personality classification to purposefully remind you of your destiny and your life purpose on earth.

Most of us tend to develop a reactionary relationship to astrology. If, for example your star sign is Gemini and everyone says that Geminis are intelligent and adaptable, if you then find yourself to be someone who is intelligent and adaptable, you may reason that it is so because you are a Gemini. You might say to your friends "I'm a typical Gemini: intelligent and adaptable".

But what if, for your incarnation here on earth, you chose to born under a specific star sign because being born under that star sign leaves you important clues to help you understand the life you have already chosen for yourself. Instead of saying to your friends "I'm a typical Gemini: intelligent and adaptable", you now tell them "I chose to be born under the star sign of Gemini to remind myself that I have chosen the qualities of intelligence and adaptability necessary for my lifetime here."

Similarly, with the Chinese twelve animal and five element systems of astrological classification, the Mayan Tzolkin calendar or the Feng Shui 9 Star Ki astrology.

From my own experience, I have found that if you apply your birthdate to the various systems of astrological classification, you will discover the personality traits you have already chosen for yourself because they are the ones which are necessary for you to have in order for you to live your life in accordance with the life you chose for yourself to have here.

For example, if I apply my birthdate to the Chinese five-element personality classification, I discover that I am strong in the elements of earth and fire (one's self and one's parents), average in wood (career) and weak in metal and water (children and money). When I apply my birthdate to the Mayan Tzolkin classification of kin or personality type, I discover I am Yellow Spectral Human, a bridge between the human realm and the realm of the light. And here I am. An author of two books, based on my journey into self-understanding, the understanding of the lives of my parents and the understanding of life in general through energy work and spiritual development. I never married and I don't have any children. I don't live in a big house and my bank account isn't overflowing into the Cayman Islands. The systems of astrological classification describe my life and my personality perfectly. Yet, I did not become the person I am today nor alter the person I had become on the discovery of these astrological systems. I only discovered them in my forties and by then, my life had already taken shape.

If you wish to verify how I have just described myself above in the Chinese five element or Mayan systems, here are my birthdate details: born 19 June 1962 at 04:20am (GMT) in Dublin, Ireland, six degrees west. It's far more interesting, however, when you google these astrological systems yourself and apply your own birthdate details instead.

A wider destiny and an even greater reward.

As spiritual beings, love is the only emotion we are allowed to feel and to feel it we have created this earth.

Of course, we are not only here on earth to fulfil our career destiny. We also choose to come here to have a particular emotional experience we cannot have in our spiritual form: the emotional experience of love.

Opening your heart and feeling love while being here on earth is both literally and symbolically *the word made flesh*.

The key to love and the key to life.

This answer about love being the key to life came in a meditation I did in Vienna on 16 February 2012. Although the answer applies to my own personal set of circumstances, it is general enough in its approach to apply to almost anyone reading this book, so I would like to share it as a piece of general wisdom and guidance for all. Read it as if it is meant for you.

I came here with the easiest task of all: to love my mother. This is the key as to why life on earth can be so easy, so rewarding.

When I love my mother, everything else falls into place. I love everything else. Who I am. What I do. Where I go. Who I am with.

The way to God is through an open heart. The way to open your heart is to love your mother.

Accept your mother's love in whatever form it takes. Even if within your mother's love there is a lot of pain.

It may also be for you that it is your own mother you have to love in order to find the key to life, or it could be your father instead, or maybe both. Regardless of which, the general advice of loving your parents to being the key to life is invaluable. The key to my life was to love my mother but after the start we had together it proved more difficult than anticipated.

For some of us, loving our parents has come easily. For some of us, not so easily. So, what to do when the key to life, through the loving of our parents, gets blocked by hurt or adversity?

Where and how to find love when your life hasn't gone according to plan.

For some of us who experience adversity in early life, we may find that that adversity not only blows us off our own particular destiny path but it also blows us off the normal, everyday life path that most people have of growing up in a happy family, doing well at school, getting a good job, finding a loving partner to share life with and starting a family of their own. We get blown off that straight and easy road onto a road that seemingly keeps having unexpected turns, dead ends and very, very bumpy bits. It can be a very tiring road to take, especially if we don't have any GPS or satnav to help us out, but the good news is is that there is a satnav, there is a map to follow, there is a blueprint for a way to get through life when life doesn't go according to plan. What this way is was revealed to me in a dream I had in January 2014.

> This was the plan. There was me and two other workers. We were starting our day in the basement of a building, collecting our gear, everything we needed. We went up through the second and third floors of the building to the fourth floor where we find and go through door 4A. The door leads into a classroom, for we are in a school

building, at the back of which is a stairwell that leads up to the roof.

Once we ascend through the stairwell, we come out onto a moor. We walk along a path, crossing the moor, until we come to a point where we assemble something using some of our tools and equipment, after which we continue onwards and upwards towards our final assembly, a transmission station, which is our goal.

We make this journey a couple of times, so I know the way to go.

This morning we start off again. However, this time it takes me longer to gather my things. I have a little more to collect than usual. The room is dark. It is before light, before dawn. We have to leave before it gets light but I am not yet ready. My workmates leave without me. I am not overly concerned as I know the way.

However, I am delayed further. I cannot tie my left shoelace. It is dark and I cannot see it properly. I am carrying more equipment, including an extra roll of razor wire on my left arm. By the time I get my shoelace done, it is dawn, it is light. One or two people come into the room, including a smiling, knowing, female face.

I have to leave the room but I also know that I have left some mess behind which needs to be tidied up. I am not happy in me to leave it for this other person to clean up, although she doesn't appear to mind. I set off on my way.

Although the journey is meant to be upwards through the school building to the floor where 4A is, I find

> myself exiting the school building and crossing over to an adjoining church, where I go around to the rear and enter through the sacristy doors.
>
> It's not the way I went before with my workmates but still it somehow brings me out onto the correct floor in the school where 4A is. I am now in a bit of a hurry. School is starting soon and I have to be out of the building before school starts. However, I cannot find 4A. I go past all the 4th form classroom doors and come to the 5th form classrooms. When I see the number 5 on the doors I know I have gone too far, so I head back down the corridor looking for 4A.

This was a dream I had in January 2014, when I was fifty-one, and it summarises my life perfectly. Things got messy at the beginning of my journey. I wasn't able to move normally through the second and third stages of my life: early and late childhood, schooling and employment. I had difficulty finding and opening my heart, as symbolised by the door 4A, and the only way I could find it was to follow a spiritual pursuit, such as meditation, as symbolised by the church, which many people in my position do. Meditation, however, leads you to go a bit too high, as symbolised by the 5th form classroom doors, so you need to come back down. You need to come back down into your body from spirit and into your heart; door 4A. The 4 represents the fourth chakra, the place in your body where you store the energy and love of your heart.

Additional symbols in the dream:

The building. It symbolises the (your) physical body.

The school. We're all here to learn.

The basement of the building. Where we start our journey. Also means our first chakra.

The room that is dark. The womb.

The transmission station. The process of ascension after death.

And the answer? Always the same. Door 4A.

Find the door to your heart and open it.

When I started my own journey of healing, however, even the idea of loving my mother, which was the key to my happiness, filled me with outrage and anger. I remember once writing down the reasons why I hated her so much. Two A4 pages of reasons. That was how much I loved my mother.

At the time, the only places I was able to find and express any kind of love were when I was either talking to the Buddha in a temple in Chiang Mai, working with my teacher to open up my spiritual centres in my sixth and seventh chakras*, which resulted in my being able to 'see the light' or then later, while sitting in meditation in my room, using meditation to go back into my spiritual centres where I could once again be able to see and connect with the light.

Of the three, meditation became the most accessible way for me to find love. In the calm of meditation, I was able to find a place where there was no hurt. I could sit with the feeling of the light in my mind and grow to feel that being in the light wasn't going to hurt me. Feeling that the light, or the spirit in the light, wasn't going to hurt me, I found a place where I could begin to trust. Although I was still unable to trust people, I was now, at least, able to trust the light. The trust and acceptance I found in meditation slowly opened the doors of trust and acceptance in my heart. These were the first openings in my heart that led to feelings and experiences of love.

It was easy to stay in a state of spiritual love in meditation but after five or six years of doing so, I began to have dreams of walking across Antarctica through heavy drifts of snow which got deeper and deeper, slowing my way forward more and more until I couldn't go on any further. The message in these dreams was simple: turn back, you have gone too far. It was time to come back down from the spiritual world, the 5th form classroom doors, and come back into earthly life, the 4th form classroom doors. It was time to test the opening of my heart in the real world and to turn spiritual love into earthly love.

Finding 4A.

Then, on 2 July 2019, I had the following dream.

> I am in a small mafia-style gang. People are chasing after us. Maybe it is because we have something valuable other people want or maybe it is because we are a bunch of crooks and we have just robbed a bank and we are in the middle of our getaway
>
> Anyway.
>
> In our attempt to get away from the people chasing us, we run down and into an underground metro station. In one of the passages in the station, me and two others, who are at the back of the gang, turn around and engage with the people following us. It is our job to defend the gang from attack at the rear. As we begin to defend ourselves, we get separated from the rest of the gang as they are still running away from the people chasing us.

After quite a lengthy fight with our pursuers, which included them trying to squeeze a liquid on us, the last of them becomes too injured to continue his pursuit of us. The rest of his colleagues have been killed. I have lost my colleagues too. There is only me left. Behind our pursuers, the entrance to the metro station has become blocked by rubble, so no one else can get in. With the threat of attack now over, I set off to catch up with the rest of my gang. But they are now very far ahead.

I run through the white-tiled metro passageways. On and on for what feels like days and days. There is scattered rubble everywhere. I never stop running but the effort of running is making me tired. I feel myself getting heavier and heavier and more and more tired. But I do not stop.

Finally, I come to a crossroads. There is a turn to the left. And at the end of the turn to the left, there is a stairway which ascends to the right. I glimpse some light at the top of the stairway, it's sunlight, and I catch a fleeting glimpse of a shadow moving at the top of the stairway. The shadow of my gang as they reach the sunlight. I have finally caught up with them. I have finally caught up with my gang. I have finally reconnected to my gang, to the rest of me.

And so, I finally find the entrance to door 4A, as described in the first dream as a stairwell that leads out onto a moor and now as a stairway ascending to the sunlight. The story in both dreams is almost identical.

The wisdom contained in these dreams is infallible and this is why I love dreams and why I encourage you to take note or journal your dreams because once you know how to interpret the symbols in your dreams, you unlock the knowledge held in both your subconscious (information relating to the patterns of behaviour you inherit from your parents, or the patterns of behaviour you develop in life due to your early childhood) and your unconscious (your spiritual self, which contains information about your destiny, your future and about life in general) and this is all you will ever need for the rest of your life.

Remember, the teacher who knows what is best for you is the teacher who knows you the best and who has been with you all along your journey: yourself.

* For a short overview and explanation of the chakras, please visit the Appendix section at the back of this book.

Opening and growing love in a heart that has been hurt.

It's a bit like setting out for a drive in your car when you only have a tiny bit of petrol in the tank. When you only have a tiny bit of love in your heart, you have to find a level of love to open out to which matches what is in your heart and will not exhaust your supply of love too quickly. So, start small and be gentle and patient with yourself.

There are lots of different kinds of little loves you can explore and play with to see if your heart opens to them.

The love for beautiful things, such as nature, art or music.

The love for small creatures, such as the birds and the bees, butterflies and ladybirds, a pet hamster or a pet rabbit.

The love of simple pleasures, such as watching a good movie or reading a good book, meeting up with friends for a Saturday lunch, the taste and texture of a square of chocolate melting in your mouth, breathing in the perfume of a beautiful rose or that day in spring when you first feel the warmth of the sun on your skin.

These are all expressions of love, so see how happy the little things in life can make you feel and let the love for little things water your heart and help it grow.

If you do try to do the big things with your heart when there is only very little love in it, you may find you will quickly exhaust yourself and you may find yourself in a situation where love is being demanded and expected of you but it's no longer there for you to give.

It can sometimes be very difficult to attain the big loves in life, such as the love necessary for a long and happy relationship or the love necessary to become a loving parent, when you have experienced such hurt in your life that it has left very little love in your own heart. It is not impossible, just difficult. But by starting small, you position yourself to grow your love into a much bigger one. Sometimes what also happens is that life smiles on you and you can meet someone who has enough love in their heart to heal you of your hurt and who will give you so much love that it fills your heart enough to be able to love them back and to be able to start and love a family of your own. And sometimes you can take a chance: take a chance on someone, or take a chance on having a baby in the hope it works out and low-and-behold, it does! Many people who have started out with very little love in their lives go on to become very happy, very successful and very loving people, bringing up children of their own who grow to have big hearts themselves and who then go on to have very loving families of their own. It's really wonderful to see.

Summary.

The spiritual side of life can be enormously helpful in the healing of your life. By connecting to your own inner spiritual self, where you store your spiritual wisdom, you can see your life circumstances and those of the people around you from a different, higher or more enlightened angle. This works to expand your conscious understanding of the circumstances of your life. It helps you to see that those who hurt you did not always intend to hurt you, that it was never their plan to hurt you but something happened to them in their lives which caused their lives and their plans to change. Your spiritual self will also guide you back to the time when there was no hurt in your life and will help you bring that time of no hurt into the present moment where you can use it to heal your life today.

Your spiritual self also contains the blueprint of your life, the life plan you drew up for yourself, just before you were born. This is the life you are meant to be living and by connecting to it, through any form of spiritual development, you position and empower yourself to reclaim that life back for yourself. To give you the correct guidance, strength and support to help you reclaim and live that life, your spiritual self also chose a spiritual family, spiritual friends and spiritual helpers to help you along your way. They all know what is right for you and they will guide you lovingly and correctly to the right place and the right thing for you. They are here for you every day and for the rest of your life.

That's the way spirit works. Spirit is here to help you. That is its reason for being. It is like having a source of clean, pure, powerful, positive energy beside you every day. All you have to do is to connect to it and use it. If you want to connect to it but don't know how, there are lots of people here to help.

Part Three.

Manifestation.

Before we start.

The third part of this book concerns manifestation. Although it is placed as the third and final part of the book, it does not imply that manifestation is the third and final part of self-healing. The three parts to self-healing as outlined in this book: Healing, Realignment and Manifestation do not necessarily occur one after the other in a linear fashion. Before completing the cycle of healing as outlined in the first part of the book, you can already be embarking on discovering and aligning yourself to your destiny self and manifesting that self. You don't have to complete the first part of healing before starting the second part and then the third. All the three aspects of self-healing can and often do run concurrently.

Accordingly, this part of the book can be read either in sequence as the third part of self-healing, or out of sequence or even independently of the rest of the book as a stand-alone discussion on manifestation.

Energetically, however, this part of the book, if read in sequence, can feel a bit like taking a step back. Part one, Healing, ends on the point of self-empowerment, revolution and change, whereas part three, Manifestation, starts with a cautious investigation of things to look out for before reaching that point of change. In a way, this part of the book could be inserted into the middle of the first part on healing, but to do so would destroy the energy flow and growing power of that part as it moves towards its culmination. So, Manifestation is offered here, editorially in the correct place, but in energy or tone, maybe feeling a little different.

Preparation: things to look out for that can block your way forward.

Manifestation is very important to a lot of people. It is often seen as a proof of success that you have reconnected to your life path and that, by doing so, the universe is providing you with all the things you need for a successful manifestation of that life.

Almost every modern self-help book makes reference to manifestation. Gurus, teachers, life coaches, therapists and healers all offer tips and guidance on the subject. Millions is being made from offering advice on manifestation, yet millions are not manifesting after following all the advice offered. Something is amiss. Something is out of alignment between the advice being offered for successful manifestation and the practice of successful manifestation. But what?

What's missing is that the advice being offered lacks the understanding of the individual life circumstances of the people seeking that advice. This is perfectly understandable. How could any teacher or guru understand the individual life circumstances of each and every one of their followers or readers? They don't. But you do. So, this is where you, the reader, the individual come into play. Your role in the art of manifestation is to take the advice being offered and to see how well it fits with your current life circumstances. You have to examine where you are in your life at the moment to see if you are truthfully ready and able to start on the path to manifestation or to see if there are any external influences, such as the people around you, that may be thwarting you in your efforts to manifest. Because, if there are, it may be that you have to deal with those issues first before you start out towards manifestation. Be aware, too, that some of the life circumstances you may have to deal with before starting out to manifest what you want can be subconscious ones, such as an already-formed subconscious belief in yourself that you do not deserve or you are not worth the abundance you are wishing to manifest. Such subconscious self-beliefs, subconscious because you are not in the present moment consciously aware of them, will act to block you in what you are consciously wanting for yourself. It is like one half of you saying "I want abundance" while your other half is silently telling you "No, you're not getting that because you don't deserve it".

It is in not addressing your life circumstances first, whether conscious or subconscious, that most often the reasons behind unsuccessful manifestation are to be found.

So, here to help you, is a list of things to reflect on before you embark on your journey towards manifestation. Each item represents a potential obstacle on your path. Read through the list to see which, if any, apply to you. Then work to resolve that issue so that it is no longer an issue. When you have removed all potential obstacles from your path, there will be nothing left in your way. You will be standing on that point of self-empowerment, revolution and change with you in total control of your destiny and direction in life.

1. You are seeking to manifest the wrong thing.

This is both obvious and not obvious. If you are asking the universe for help in manifesting something and what you are asking for is not the right thing for you, the universe is not going to send it to you.

If you are already doing something in your life which is not in alignment with your soul purpose, with what you are meant to be doing in life, and you ask the universe or a 'higher power' for help, such as in a continuing but more successful manifestation of what you are doing, the universe will first say to you: "Actually, what you are doing at the moment is not right for you. You need to change".

Similarly, if you are seeking a change from what you are currently doing and you ask the universe for help in manifesting a specific, new direction for yourself but a direction which is not in alignment with your soul purpose, the universe will similarly first say to you: "Actually, what you are asking for is not the right thing for you. You need to change what you want to something different".

Although this advice is always offered, not everyone hears it and even if you do hear it, you then have the freedom of choice whether to accept or decline it and if you decline it, to continue along the path that is leading you away from what is best for you or to choose a path that is not the right path for you to be taking.

It may be that in another year or so you again ask the universe for help in manifestation because nothing has happened since the first time you asked. But again, nothing happens. It may be that you end up asking the universe four or five times for help before you finally give up on what you have been asking for and start out on something else because what you have been asking for hasn't worked out for you. This is how the universe sometimes helps you. It doesn't give you what you ask for, because what you are asking for is not the right thing for you to be asking for. It's only when you look back at a time in your life that didn't work out the way you wanted can you understand why it didn't work out the way you wanted. You see the bigger picture. It's not always easy to see it, though, when you are in the middle of it.

This example, however, only applies if you are asking the universe or a 'higher power' for guidance. If you are sitting down with a piece of paper in front of you and using only your own conscious mind intelligence to plan your future, the whole issue of it being or not being the right thing for you does not arise. If you do not ask the universe for help, the universe does not interfere.

Giving up the day job.

The first half of my life didn't work out. It took me forty years to realise it and to finally start doing something about it. I'm a slow learner. In January 2004, at the age of forty-one, I began working with my teacher in Chiang Mai in an attempt to understand why certain aspects of my life weren't working out for me. The first theme we examined was relationships, after which came career and family. Due to visa restrictions and the fact my teacher was living in a far-off country, I was only able to visit her once a year, which meant we were only able to deal with one theme per year. First relationships, then career and then family.

During my visit to her, in January 2005, when we were examining the theme of career, my teacher guided me to bring my breathing and focus to an area of black energy in my right leg. She 'saw' the black energy there, I didn't. After a few minutes of concentrating my energy and breathing into this part of my leg, it felt to me as if I was trying to release some sort of blockage from it. A blockage, it transpired, I had been holding onto all my life to my revealing the truth about myself, to my revealing the truth about who I really am and what I should be doing in life. For some reason, I was afraid to reveal my true self to myself.

Within minutes of starting the exercise, two colours came very strongly into my mind's eye: black and sky blue.

When I told my teacher of the two colours, she told me to focus deeply into them and to ask out loud: "What is the truth behind my black and sky blue. What is it that I do not want to discover about myself?"

Within minutes, I got the answer:

I have been sent as an angel from God to heal with the power of purple.

This totally freaked me out. An angel? Sent from God? This is who I am and this is what I am meant to be doing in life? This was very new to me and, in all honesty, I didn't even know how to react to this information. It made me very uncomfortable.

When the answer was revealed, however, the colours of black and sky blue that I had been seeing in my mind's eye, immediately changed. The black disappeared, leaving only the sky blue. From the training I had already done with my teacher in energy work, I understood that the colour sky blue is the colour of the energy that is given off by words and thoughts that contain the truth, so that when I now saw only sky blue in my mind's eye, I knew that what had been revealed was the truth.

It is, however, not the easiest thing to say to someone when they ask you in a social situation:

"...So tell me, what do you do for a living?"

"Well, I'm an angel sent from God to heal with the power of purple."

Can you imagine the reaction?

Hence the black in my black and sky blue. My fear of being embarrassed or ridiculed. My fear of it being the truth.

Yet this revelation was fundamental to my future development as it showed me, albeit in very esoteric and abstract terms, that I had been following the wrong path in life and that I needed to change from someone with a normal, nine-to-five day job to someone who healed with purple.

Then later that year, in July, while working as a massage therapist at a yoga centre in Crete, the following clarification of this message came to me one afternoon, while in meditation:

My deep truth is that I have been sent as a healer. To connect to this truth and to fully understand it and manifest it, I have to connect to my intuition.

When I connect to my intuition, I will be able to use higher colours to heal, as by then I will not have to use 'hands-on' to heal.

Finally, almost twelve years later, in January 2017, I received the following message from one of my massage clients, who is a channelled-automatic writer:

My role is to use my skills and my physical energy to create the opportunity for other beings to develop and self-realise. This is my self-worth.

My wish in sharing this experience is to show you that it is possible to learn everything you need to know about your life purpose through spiritual development, meditation and clairvoyance and that you can be shown the life that is right for you in different ways, such as in the 'I have been sent as an angel' meditation I did with my teacher or the 'my role is to use my skills…' channelled message I received from one of my massage clients. Both tell the same story but through very different means. Although esoteric and spiritual in nature, both sets of advice have born very tangible, real world results.

This doesn't mean you have to know your soul purpose in order to live a fulfilled life. You don't. What it does mean, however, is that if things aren't working out for you and you ask the universe for help, it may come to you that you are not in alignment with your soul purpose and that if you work to discover the path you chose for yourself, you will then be in a much better position to be able to successfully manifest the fulfilling life you are asking for.

How do you know if what you are doing in life is the wrong thing for you to be doing?

Sometimes your spiritual self, through your unconscious mind, will try telling you that you are out of alignment with your soul purpose through the medium of your dreams. Look out for a dream in which you are going back to do a job you once had. When you go back to restart the job in your dream, it somehow doesn't feel the same as you were expecting it to be. It's not quite the same as you remember it to have been the first time around. Something about it is different and you're not as happy in doing it now as you thought you were going to be.

You might only have this dream once a year or once every two years but if you have it three or four times over a six to eight period it is showing you that what you are currently doing in your life is not exactly what you first chose for yourself to do, just before you were born. You have fallen out of alignment with what is the right thing for you to be doing, your already chosen destiny.

II. Timing.

Another important factor in the process of manifestation is timing. If you ask the universe for something and it is not the right time for that thing to be given to you, then it will not be given to you. You have to wait. Maybe there are other responsibilities you have to fulfil first, such as being with a family member who needs your help, or maybe there is something you have to learn or do before you get what you want, like understanding why things have worked out the way they have. Maybe there is a life lesson you have to learn first. The reasons surrounding timing are not always obvious and usually only reveal themselves afterwards, when you are able to look back on a particular part of your life and see that it was indeed not the right time for you to be given what you were asking for. When the time is right for you, the universe provides. If you are being frustrated by your attempts to manifest, check with someone trained in spiritual arts to see if the issue is one of timing. They will be able to tell you.

III. Someone is blocking you in your attempts to manifest.

Two types of people can block you in your attempts to manifest: those you know who are doing it and those you don't.

Those you know can be your current employer, your current spouse or one or both of your parents. They can simply turn around to you and say “No, I won't let you do that”. Because you are consciously aware of these people and the ways they are blocking you, you can take consciously-made informed decisions to counter the effects of such blocking.

What can also happen, however, is that people who you don't think are blocking you, or who you think are no longer blocking you, are, and it is their continuing control over you that is blocking you in your attempts to manifest.

Let's say, for example, you had a very controlled upbringing during which time you had to ask your parents' approval or permission for everything. Can I leave the table? Can I watch TV? Can I go out? Can I invite a friend over? Or that if you got caught doing something without their approval, such as sneaking out to go to a party, you got punished for it. Such a way to be living your life soon becomes hot-wired into you and forms a subconscious pattern of behaviour in adulthood. In adulthood, even if you are no longer living with your parents, your subconscious self will still need their approval or permission before you can do or get what you want. No longer consciously aware of this, yet wanting to change your life to the way you want it to be, you write down a list of positive affirmations and manifestations to create a positive springboard for change. You state what you want and you set yourself the way to get what you want. Yet, without your parents' approval or permission, your subconscious will stop you getting what you want until it gets your parents' permission or approval first. If you have been aware of this pattern of behaviour and you have worked to successfully release yourself from it, then you are OK. You are free to manifest and take what you want. If, however, you have not thought about this potential pattern of behaviour in you or if you have not yet fully worked to break yourself free of it, you will still be subject to it. You will not be able to get what you want until your subconscious receives approval or permission for it first.

How do you know if it is your subconscious need for parental approval that is blocking you?

Your subconscious need for approval or permission can reveal itself to you in your dreams. Look out for dreams in which you revisit situations where there was someone who approved of you, nurtured you or allowed you to do what you wanted to do. A positive force in your life. A person who trusted in you and encouraged you. This person may have been your favourite teacher at school, a supportive boss at work, an old friend or a family member outside your immediate family. Even though you may no longer be at that school or place of work or you no longer see that particular friend or family member, this person appears to you in your dreams. In your dreams, this person symbolises 'approval'. Your dream is telling you that you still seek or need approval.

The dream reveals what is holding you back from manifestation. With this information, seek out someone trained in spiritual arts and ask them to release you from your need of parental approval. It is possible, through spiritual work, to break this bond and set you free of it.

Control and ownership of you.

It is not only parents who can own or control your life like this. Anyone who did something to you that changed the course of your life to a direction you did not want or could not control also subconsciously controls part of your life from that moment on and can block your efforts in manifesting what you want today.

Claims of control and ownership can also be put on you by a domineering spouse or employer, someone who thinks they are superior to you, a bully or even a spiritual teacher in an ashram. In all instances, any claim of ownership or control over you has no grounding.

Owning or controlling another person's life is absolutely wrong. There is no reason for it, yet people give themselves a myriad of their own made up reasons for doing it, such as: I am your parent and I can do whatever I want to you. This is total falsehood. Nowhere is it recorded in any book of wisdom, truth, spirituality or parenting that a parent has the right of ownership of their children. Nowhere. It is a totally selfish, made up and false claim but because it has garnered thousands of years of practice, it is given the status of justified. This is why, when working to break any bond of control or ownership over you, you have to go to a 'power' or 'jurisdiction' that is higher than human reasoning. You have to seek help from above, from spirit, through working with someone trained in spiritual arts.

Affirmations to help break any bond of control or ownership over you.

Here are two powerful affirmations you can use when dealing with any person or entity who is interfering with, owning, or controlling your life. The first affirmation can be used when you have a sense that it is happening but you have yet to discover the identity of the controlling entity. The second affirmation can be used once you have discovered the identity of the person controlling you.

1.
To any entity trying to control me.
There is a part of me that is way above and beyond your control and way above and beyond your reach.
You know what it is. It is the truth and the light that resides inside me.
This is the part of me you know you cannot control.
So, let go, because if you cannot control that part of me, you cannot control me.
You may think you can and you certainly want me to think you can but I will use that part of me you cannot reach to show you that you cannot.

2.
I am not yours to own, O spirit who calls himself/herself [the name of the person].
I return your energy back to you.
I return to you what is yours.

Use the energy that I return to you to re-establish and strengthen your connection to yourself.

When using the second affirmation, try your best not to think of what the person, towards whom you are directing the affirmation, did to you. Thinking about what they did to you acknowledges the power they once had over you and by thinking about it again, in the now, you are bringing that power back into the present. Just imagine the face of the person you are directing the affirmation towards and simply and strongly send their energy back to them. Be as emotionally unattached as possible.

Using the white light to help break any bond of control or ownership over you.

You can also use the power of prayer to help break any bond of control or ownership that may be being exerted on you by someone else. In their abstract, energetic form, you can sometimes, in meditation, sense or see these bonds of control as thick, heavy metal chains, either extending from the area of your solar plexus, if it is someone outside your immediate family who is controlling you, or from your navel/sexual organs if it is one of your parents who is controlling you. The stronger the force of control someone is exerting over you, the bigger and thicker the chains appear. You can, in your imagination, try to break these chains. If the chains are thin and weak, this may be possible to do, but if the chains are heavy and black or silver in colour, you may need some help. If you seek help in prayer, ask for the highest and brightest source of white light to be sent to help you. You will need prayer energy, or spiritual energy of this colour and intensity to break heavy chains. Alternatively, you can work with someone in the spiritual arts to help you break free of such bonds and chains. Don't worry, it can be done.

How I use the white light to break the bonds of control and ownership in a massage client.

The brightest white light serves as the highest power or jurisdiction in determining what is truthful or baseless in human behaviour and I often use it in my healing work with clients. If I am working with a client who is being adversely affected by the controlling energy of another person, I tune in, with my mind's eye, to the controlling energy which is to be found in my client's energy system. Once I have tuned into it, I can see the face or identity of the owner of the controlling energy, the person who is exerting control over my client. Again, using my mind's eye, I make a direct connection with that person. I introduce myself to them and invite them to come with me on a journey. I bring that person with me to the white light. In the presence of the white light, I ask the controlling person a question. I ask them if it is right for them to control my client. In defence of their action of exerting control over my client they never say no. They always say yes. I then challenge them to prove it. I demand from them the proof that they have the right to control my client. I ask them to show me that their right to control my client is indeed a true right and is recorded in *The Book of Truth*, the theosophical book, similar to the *Akashic Records*, in which all things that are truthful in life are recorded. Facing the white light, I ask them to open *The Book of Truth* on the page regarding control and to show me where it states it is right and correct for one soul to own and control another. They open the page and try to show me the proof. But, of course, it isn't there. The page is blank. It is not there because it is not a true claim. It is a falsehood. It's a baseless claim made up out of nothing. Faced with the realisation of the truth of the matter and in the presence of the white light, the controlling person can no longer justify or defend their baseless belief that they have the right to control my client and so they let go. My client, in that moment, is then set free of the adverse controlling influence of the person trying to control them.

IV. You are carrying too much of another person's emotional baggage.

The other way people block you in manifesting what you want in life is by dumping their emotional baggage on you, their unresolved emotional issues, and expecting you to either sort it out for them or to carry it for them for the rest of your life. Often, they have been doing it to you for so long you are no longer aware they are doing it. Carrying other people's baggage enslaves you. It slows your life down and gets in your way of claiming the life of rich reward that is rightly yours. Instead of living the life you have already chosen for yourself, you end up living a life of picking up, sorting out, cleaning up or carrying other people's unresolved issues.

Of course, this is the way much of humanity works, especially in families and in relationships. It is expected of you to carry other people's baggage. It is even argued it is your duty to do so or that it is normal human behaviour to do so but just because it is normal human behaviour, it doesn't make it the right thing to do. Here's why.

Let's say, for example, you have had a troubled relationship with your father and that the root of this troubled relationship goes back to the trouble he had with his own father in his own childhood.

If this is the case, then how are you, as the child of your father during your own childhood, teenage or early adult years going to be able to sort this out? You're not. You can't. And the reason why you can't, is because you don't have the answer. It's that simple. And you don't have the answer because you don't have access to the full facts of the story between your father and his. Only your father and his father know the story.

But because he is your father, you want to help. You want to understand him, so you can understand your troubled relationship with him. So, you ask your father for the story of what happened between him and his father. Your father tells you the story, but the chances are it will only be his side of the story. In telling his side of the story, your father will also add on a few bits here and leave out a few bits there. That is what people do, either by accident or on purpose.

Then there will be the missing subconscious parts of the story. Bits which need to be included but aren't. There always are. These are the parts of the story concerning your grandfathers' actions towards your father which your father never understood and because he couldn't understand them, he couldn't let them go. Your grandfather probably never understood them either, which is why he couldn't stop acting them out on your father, yet they all need to be understood if the whole story is to be understood, if your father is to be free of his father and you of yours. And this understanding is to be found in the subconscious minds of your father and grandfather, not in your father's conscious-mind speculative reasoning concerning his father's behaviour.

So, what you get is 50% of a story, filed down to 40% through adjustment and then filed down a further 10% due to the omission of the subconscious details. What you are left with is 30% of a story and how on earth can you understand any situation if only 30% of that situation is revealed to you. You cannot.

The only two people who can sort it out are your father and his father and all you can do is to point your father in that direction. If he doesn't want to go there, then you are stuck until the next time you try to point him in that direction. If he cannot go there because there is no contact between him and his father, there is still a way forward. There are a range of available family therapies, such as family constellation work, in which one of the protagonists does not need to be present in order for their story to be told and resolved. There is also the spiritual arts route, through the work of a medium or clairvoyant who can, while acting as an intermediary, establish a link of communication between your father and his father, so that your father can talk to his father in spirit. Your grandfather doesn't need to be present. Nor does it matter if he is living or has passed away.

The way through.

Paradoxically, if you stand up to the 'I dump my baggage on you because my parents did it to me' pattern of behaviour and say:

"No, I am not taking this anymore. Sort your own stuff out", you will probably be judged weak, selfish and running away from responsibility.

Similar to what I wrote earlier about other people owning and controlling you, nowhere it is recorded in any book of wisdom, truth or spirituality that anyone has the right to dump their emotional baggage onto another being and then expect them to either sort it out for them or to carry it for them for the rest of their lives. It is, yet again, a totally made up and baseless claim, but because it has garnered thousands of years of practice, it is given the status of accepted and justified. This is why, when working to break the bond of other people dumping their baggage on you, you also have to go to a jurisdiction or a power that is higher than human reasoning. You have to seek help from above, from spirit.

You may also need to break away from your current life for a while, so you can re-establish and strengthen your personal boundaries, which are gifted to everyone and which are there to protect you against other people dumping their baggage on you. Once you have re-established and strengthened your boundaries, you will have created the extra space and freedom necessary in you for you to focus on your own life, while, at the same time, still being attentive and supportive of others.

In sharing this example, I am not suggesting you act one way or the other. I am simply laying it out the way it is. If you are aware of the 'I dump my baggage on you' pattern of behaviour in your family and you are OK with it either because you love your family dearly or because it has never been too much of an issue for you, then stay where you are and just skip this item in the book.

Nor am I suggesting you walk away from someone who really needs you.

There is a difference between people who need your help and people who manipulate you into helping them because they are not motivated enough to help themselves. In the latter case, you represent the easy way out for such people and as long as you are around, they will choose the easy way out.

So, not for a single moment am I suggesting you walk away from someone who sincerely needs your help. You do not walk away from a sick or helpless child, parent, sibling, spouse or friend. If you are looking to make a new or better life for yourself while you are in the phase of your life when you need to be looking after someone else, it will be revealed to you that now is not the right time for you to receive those gifts and that you will have to wait a little while longer to get them because you have other tasks to complete first. In such instances, the block to your manifestation is timing. You have other responsibilities to fulfil first.

V. You don't actually want things to go well for you.

This applies if you are someone who has had to struggle or work hard all your life. Although your life struggles have been a real pain, you have somehow ended up wearing your ability to get through tough times as a badge of honour. It is not that you enjoy the struggle but that you have somehow built a sense of identity and self-worth from having gotten through those tough times. You are a survivor and you wear your survivor's badge with a sense of pride. Now tired of the struggle, however, you finally want things to go well for you. You want a better, easier life.

Then, let's say, one morning your plumbing bursts in the

kitchen. You can't afford a plumber to come and fix it, so you set yourself the whole day to fix it yourself. You work out a list of all the replacement parts and tools you will need to get the job done. You know your plumbing is old. You may not get everything you need straight away, so you set yourself up for a long day of visiting different DIY and plumbing supply stores. You set yourself up for the struggle. It is, after all, what you're used to.

You call into the first DIY store on your list. The one nearest you, which you don't think will have everything you need. But it does. And within minutes you have it all. Your day has been made easy. But you weren't expecting that. You were expecting a day of struggle. Instead, you have been given everything you need straight away. But what is the fun in that? You had your whole day planned ahead of you but now your plan is ruined and your day is over. What is the fun in having everything given to you on a plate straight away? Where is the challenge in that? There is no survivor badge to be awarded for that and no 'what a terrible day I had' story to tell your friends afterwards.

You ask for things to go better in your life, yet when it is given to you, you ask: what is the fun in that? You actually resist, or push it away from you.

If you can catch yourself in a moment like this, it is a real eye-opener. You realise that from deep inside you, you don't want the easy life. You actually prefer the struggle.

However, in that moment, you also have the power to change it. You realise you have a resistance to things going well for you, so now change that resistance. Begin to tell yourself that there's nothing wrong in having things working out easily for you. Begin to change your mindset. Give thanks that things have begun to go well and teach yourself to enjoy it. Forget the 'I am a survivor' badge. Let that go. You're done with that.

The more you give thanks for things working out well for you, the more things will work out well for you.

Similarly, if you are someone who does not like receiving help from others, then how is it going to work out for you when you begin to ask the universe to send you help by manifesting something good or positive in your life? You need to be honest with yourself when you reflect on the following questions: Do I resist it when other people offer me help? Do I not like being helped? Am I happier doing everything by myself? If so, then you will similarly but subconsciously resist help from the universe when it is sent to you, even if you consciously ask for it.

In you do find yourself in such circumstances, then you have to begin to open yourself to receiving help. Start by using and repeating this simple affirmation:

I am open to the idea of receiving.

I am open to the idea of receiving help.

And then when you feel more comfortable:

I am open to receiving.

I am open to receiving help.

I know it can be difficult to suddenly be open to receiving help when, possibly for years, you have been resisting it. So, give it time. Start gently. Just be open to the idea. Nothing more. Then let it progress. Naturally and organically. When the postman comes delivering the package you want, you have to open the door in order to receive it!

VI. Something frightening from your past is holding you back.

This applies to people who have experienced an acutely frightening experience in their lives, such as having their survival seriously threatened and who have yet to fully process and release the fear they are still holding in themselves relating to that event.

An acutely frightening event in your life is usually something you are very much aware of because you remember it and you have probably already taken steps to help yourself come to terms with it and resolve it.

Sometimes, however, your life can have been seriously threatened, yet, in adulthood you have no recollection of it happening. This is usually something that happened in your earliest infancy or while you were still in your mother's womb. Although you have no recollection of the event in question, a remaining ghost of the fear you experienced throughout the event as it happened to you is still residing in your body.

Fear does not stop you from being able to manifest. The purpose of fear is to slow you down. Light amounts of fear, such as a sense of caution, are actually very positive and only slow you down a very little. Chronic or acute amounts of fear, on the other hand, can slow you down to a crawl, but even when you are totally overcome with fear, such as in sleep paralysis, some part of you will still be able to move. Fear doesn't have the power to stop or block you completely.

When you have large amounts of residual fear in your body, you tend to move through life more slowly. You are afraid of anything that moves or shakes you too dynamically and that can even include too many good things happening to you too quickly within the process of positive manifestation. As a result, it is not unusual to end up being too afraid to manifest what you want in life, even though you want to. This doesn't mean you will always be unable to manifest what you want in life, it just means that if you do want to manifest a rewarding life for yourself, you may need more time and extra support and encouragement from family, friends and loved ones.

VII. You are facing the wrong direction for manifestation.

When wanting to manifest something good for yourself, the flow of life's energy around you should be towards you. The thing you want to manifest should be able to flow freely to you so you can integrate with it. Therefore, the flow of your own energy should support this flow.

People sometimes wish to manifest something good for themselves at a time in their lives when there is not much good happening. Sometimes you have just come through a bad patch and you now want to manifest something good for yourself, however you are still in the phase of letting go or moving on from the bad patch, so the flow of energy around you is one of letting go and of things moving away from you and not towards you, which it needs to be for manifestation.

Similarly, some people wish to manifest something good at a time in their lives when they are worried about the future. When you are worried about the future, you tend not to move. You tend to hold on to where you are and to what you've got. You don't want anything to change as you are afraid that any change will bring about something unfavourable, such as a job loss or an increase in your utilities bill. You batten down the hatches. In such a situation, you halt the flow of energy around you. Everything stagnates. Energy is neither gravitating towards you nor moving away from you and it needs to be gravitating towards you for manifestation. For you to want a good future, you have to be open to the possibilities of the future but if you are worried about the future, then you are not open to it.

It just so happens that sometimes when you wish for manifestation, you block the flow of the energy necessary for manifestation because there is something bigger, or more important going on around you at the time.

Wanting to manifest. Trying to let go the past. Being worried about the future. You can be doing all three at the same time, yet their energy flows run contrary to each other. One hinders the flow of the other. It's like being in your car and trying to turn left, right and go straight ahead all at the same time. You have to do one manoeuvre at a time and in the correct order in order to progress more easily in the direction you desire, not all three together.

So, when you are trying to manifest, look at your life and see if you are worried about anything or if you are trying to move on from something.

Maybe you need to do one thing first, then the next and then, finally, the manifestation, when you can apply all your focus on it, enabling it to come to you more easily and more quickly.

This is not to say that it is impossible to manifest when you are, for example, worried about the future, it is just to say that it is more difficult. Just make yourself aware that if what you are trying to manifest for yourself isn't happening quickly enough for you, it may be because you are worried about the future, so give yourself a little more time.

Similarly, if you are someone who has been in the role of helper or carer for many years, it will be difficult for you when you start asking the universe for help. This is because, traditionally, help has flowed away from you instead of towards you and now you are asking for that flow to be reversed. If this is the case, you may have to lessen, pause or even end your role as a helper and instead begin to open yourself to being someone who is helped. Start by setting the intention of reversing the flow of help energy towards you instead of away from you. You can start with a simple affirmation, such as:

I am open to the idea of help flowing towards me.

I am open to the idea of help flowing towards me from the universe.

And then, when you feel things beginning to shift:

I am open to help flowing to me.

I am open to help flowing to me from the universe.

Changing the flow of energy from moving away from you to moving towards you takes time. It is a bit like a supertanker in open water doing a 180° turn. So, be patient. It might take a few months. The good news, however, is that as soon as you start with a sincere intention for change, your intention will trigger the change.

VIII. You are going through a period of karmic reparation.

Reparation is making amends for your past indiscretions. Giving something back, as it were. Karmic reparation is making amends for past indiscretions in your past lives. It is making amends in this, your current lifetime, for indiscretions you made but have no conscious recollection of, in your previous lifetimes. Sometimes, you can unknowingly be going through a period of karmic reparation and during such a period, you will not be allowed to manifest or accumulate more-than-necessary wealth or happiness for yourself. This is because you are not meant to have more than the necessary wealth and happiness for yourself.

Karmic reparation is not an easy-to-recognise phenomenon. Very few people when they are going through one say to their friends "Yeah, I'm just going through a period of karmic reparation at the moment", but just because it is not easy to recognise, it doesn't mean that it is impossible to recognise. A period of karmic reparation has specific characteristics, which, when you are going through one, are not too difficult to spot once you know what to look for.

Signs that show you are going through a period of karmic reparation.

1. What you are doing in life at the moment can be described as doing something that brings good to other people.

2. It was not a conscious choice of yours to end up doing what you are doing. What you have ended up doing somehow came to you. You stumbled into it, rather than you seeking it out in the first place.

3. Although you are doing good for other people, what you are doing isn't making you feel good about yourself while doing it. It doesn't give you any feelings of self-satisfaction or pride, nor does it give you the buzz other people in your area of work appear to get from doing the same thing.

4. Although you are good at what you do, your business never grows beyond a certain level no matter how hard you try. Nor does your work bring you strong financial reward, other than just covering your basic needs plus maybe a little extra.

Reparation is a bit like saying the ten Hail Marys you are given after confessing your wrongdoings in Confession. Saying the Hail Marys is doing an act of good but it's not necessarily designed to make you feel good while doing it. Nor do you get paid for doing it. It's penance.

How long a period of reparation lasts depends on what you are making reparation for and at what age in your life it starts depends on what age you chose for it to start. You choose when to start a period of reparation when you are going through the details of your destiny just before you are born. Of course, not everyone chooses, or is destined to serve a period of reparation in their life.

If you find you may be going through a period of reparation, seek out someone trained in the spiritual arts and ask them to break or cancel any karmic contracts you are making reparation for. I would have if I had known what I was dealing with. Karmic reparation held me back for fourteen years and I wouldn't want it doing the same to you.

IX. Subconsciously, you don't believe you are worthy enough to get what you want.

Manifesting what you want in life is the same as getting your reward for your efforts in trying to manifest what you want in life.

In wanting to manifest something good for yourself, you are setting a reward for yourself. So, if you are unable to manifest what you want, it might be showing you that you are unable to get your reward for your efforts in manifestation. Someone or something is blocking you from getting your reward. You are suffering reward block.

This blockage, like all other forms of subconscious blockage, is rooted in your earliest childhood or infancy, when something you felt you deserved as a reward for your efforts in a particular matter was not given to you.

As a newborn, infant or a young child, when you are denied a reward you feel you deserve, the reason you give yourself for not being given that reward is very simple:

I am not worthy enough to get what I deserve.

And when you are then given a poorer substitute for the reward you feel you deserve, it forms the additional self-belief:

I am only worthy of (getting) second-best.

These are not consciously deduced reasons, in the way adults deduce reason. These are underdeveloped, unreasoned deductions in the way infants deduce reason. And in 100% of cases, the reason an infant gives themselves for not getting what they feel they deserve, their reward, is wrong. It's the way infantile reasoning works and if it is not corrected in infancy, it remains uncorrected into adulthood. The adult, still (subconsciously) believing they are not worthy enough to get their reward, now in the form of manifesting something good for themselves, will (subconsciously) block themselves from getting their reward, in order to fit that (subconscious) belief, and instead will accept or settle for less, in order to fit their other (subconscious) belief. And because all this happens on the subconscious level, the person is totally unaware that they are doing it to themselves.

The theme of unworthiness is universal and, from my experience, is the biggest, single reason why adults are unable to manifest what they want. I had it and I know many of my friends and colleagues had it too.

Unworthiness is tricky, because like everything else in your subconscious, you're not consciously aware of it. You don't realise it's there, yet you feel its effects. Unworthiness is the unanswerable answer to the question: "What's stopping you?" You don't know the answer because you don't have the answer. But someone else does. It's like when someone steals a pair of socks from you and then when you go looking for them, you can't find them and you don't understand why you can't find them. Your attempt to find your socks is being blocked, not by you, but by someone else. Then when your spouse or one of your parents asks you

"Why can't you find your socks?" (what's stopping you (from manifesting what you want)), you can't answer. Only the person who stole your socks can, because they are the only person who knows why. You don't. But, of course, there are ways of finding out.

Unworthiness is also the hidden cause of self-sabotage, when you uncontrollably do something to cause things to go wrong when things have been going well for you.

The first part to healing unworthiness is in finding out what you first sought as a reward in your life, from whom you sought that reward and if it was denied you, why. Then, when you understand why, you can correct your thinking related to the event from: 'I didn't get what I wanted because I thought I was unworthy' to 'I didn't get what I wanted because (the true reason)', so correcting your belief in your unworthiness.

The second part is in building your self-worth anew from the moment you correct your misbelief in your unworthiness. You can do this in a number of ways:

You can use positive affirmations such as:

(From this moment on,) I am worthy (of getting the reward I deserve and want).

This breaks the flow of the energy of unworthiness from your past into your present. By breaking this flow, you are more quickly able to turn unworthiness into worthiness. Think of it as cold water, warm water and hot water. Let's say you have been filling your kitchen sink with water from the cold tap but now you want the water to be warm, so you turn on the hot tap. Hot water starts to be added, but if you do not turn off the cold tap, it is going to take much longer to make the water warm. So, you turn off the cold tap. You turn off the flow of unworthiness from the past to facilitate the flow of worthiness in the present.

In addition, you can use positive visualisations to support your affirmations, such as the 'gold box in your heart' visualisation, as described on pages 101-102. This doubles the strength of your growing sense of self-worth in you.

The other great thing you can do is to start practising the 'thank you as a prelude to self-love' exercise, as described on pages 76-78. These three things together: positive affirmation, positive visualisation and self-love work to create a very powerful force in the building of self-worth.

In short, self-worth can be healed. It is all about building it anew in the present, while understanding, forgiving and letting go the events in the past that negatively impacted it.

The root of my own subconscious unworthiness.

I discovered the root of my own unworthiness from a meditation I did at the yoga centre where I worked in Crete, in August 2009. These are the notes I journaled immediately following the meditation:

> The first time I felt unworthy and not being able to receive what I deserved was when my mother gave me the bottle instead of her breast. To be breastfed was my reward for my effort in being born. This made me very angry as I had no choice but to accept a substitution for what I really wanted and it set in motion the greater and longer-lasting feelings of unworthiness and not being worthy enough to get what I deserve and always settling for a (poorer) substitute.

By the time I did this meditation, I had already done several years of self-examination and energy work with my teacher in Chiang Mai, so I was well used to the process of recalling memories and experiences that were held deeply within my subconscious. I would not expect you to receive this level of revelation from a meditation if you have only just started to meditate yourself but with a little practice it will come! Alternatively, you can do as I did and work with someone trained in the spiritual arts to help you uncover the root of any lack of self-worth you may feel you have.

Nowadays when I talk to my mother in my meditations and prayers, I can ask her: "Am I worthy?" and she always replies: "Yes". This works to heal my belief in my unworthiness at source.

Not being breastfed lay at the root of my own, personal subconscious belief in unworthiness. The circumstances in which it happened and the reasons my mother had for not breastfeeding me were very particular to my life and will not apply to yours in any way, which is why if you were not breastfed yourself, it may not have caused you any feelings of unworthiness.

X. Grounding.

Abundance comes with grounding.

Grounding is being happy with who you are, where you are, who you are with and what you are doing. The happier you are with these things, the more grounded you are. If you are not fully grounded, there will be a degree of internal conflict or resistance within you and if there is internal resistance within you, there will be internal resistance within you to manifestation. It is harder to manifest if there are one or two aspects of your life you are not happy with. Not impossible, just more difficult.

So, to help you in your efforts towards a more successful manifestation of what you want, here are some steps you can take to help ground yourself more strongly and so help abundance come more easily to you. Firstly, where you are.

Where you are.

Look to where you are living. The house you are living in. The town you are living in. Your local environment. If you are not happy where you are living or with the people you are living with, if, for example, you are living in shared accommodation, see if you can move to a different, preferred location, somewhere you would like to live. If this is not possible, see if you can find something or somewhere about your local environment that you do like. This could be a park, a sports club, a coffee shop or a church. Somewhere you can go to, feel good in, feel part of and call it yours. Somewhere where you feel you belong. "This is my favourite place." "This is my club." "This is where I like to come for a coffee on Saturdays." Once you are happy to call somewhere yours, you are beginning to attach yourself to that place. You are beginning to throw down roots there. You are beginning to ground yourself there. The more places you can call yours, the more grounded you become.

If there is nothing you like about your local environment, then find somewhere you do like. This can often be in nature. The ocean, the mountains, the forests or just some part of the country that is particularly beautiful to you. Maybe somewhere you have been before that triggered a deep happiness in you or where you felt a connection or where you felt your feet sink deeply into the ground. Always note somewhere where you feel your feet sinking deeply into the ground. These are places that are right or good for you to be in and are where you can ground yourself easily and strongly.

Go to these places. Go back to these places. Even if you live hundreds of miles away, once you visit such a place and feel a connection to it, you can go back home and still maintain that connection. In your mind, in your thoughts, you can draw a grounding line from where you are living to that place and you can send all your energies, all your hurts, all your sorrows along that line to be grounded in the place where you found connection. Grounding by proxy! It works. When I first moved to Austria, I continued to ground myself through my former connection to New Zealand. It is, however, not a permanent solution to grounding. You can't always be living in one place and be grounding yourself through another. That creates conflict within you. It's like living in two places at the same time. Grounding by proxy is a temporary solution until you are able to ground yourself where you are.

If you still can't think of any place where you could go to ground yourself, try visiting someone working in the spiritual arts. Someone who can connect you to someone in their spirit form, such as your guardian angel or a deceased former loved one. Someone who has always known what is best for you and who can see what is best for you from where they are now. They'll tell you where to go. All you need do is ask them. I did this when I first moved to Austria. I visited a medium-clairvoyant who gave me the message to seek out places where the trees had needles on their branches instead of leaves.

What you are doing.

Look, also, to where you work. OK, so not so many people like what they do or where they work but if you do, then use your love of what you do or where you work as your way to ground yourself. There can be enormous pride in what you do and what you achieve at work. Use it to create an identity for yourself. An identity that will give you the necessary autonomy to ground yourself. You may have a bit of difficulty establishing your identity or individual place within your family or within your local environment, but, if among your co-workers you are seen to be damn fine worker, then a damn fine worker is who you are!

If there is nothing to like about what you do or where you work, find a hobby, or a personal interest you do like, preferably something that has a strong social or community aspect and preferably something you might have dabbled in when you were younger. This could be anything from dancing to playing sport, reading graphic novels or collecting things. The more time and effort you put into developing your hobby, the more you will ground yourself. You may not be happy with the type of job you have but if you're a damn fine salsa dancer who everyone wants to partner with, then a damn fine salsa dancer is who you are!

Who you are with.

Who you are with and changing who you are with is more tricky to deal with as who you are with includes your parents, siblings, children, spouse, partner, lovers, friends, work colleagues, fellow students and the people living in your local community. How happy you are with these people is a question only you can answer. All I can suggest, and it is always easy to do so from the outside, is to go through the list of people you are with and to see if anyone on that list is making you unhappy. Then see if it is possible in any way to break from that person, either for a short time or perhaps a longer time, or to put a strong enough border between you and that person so that, in either case, you won't be as adversely affected by them as you might have been. Alternatively, if this is not an option, see if you can, in some way, become more understanding and more accepting of the person, whether family member, long-term friend or employer, thus creating more peace and calm in your own self, regardless of the other person involved. The point of doing this exercise is simply to reduce the pressure, or weight of any negative influence another person may be having on you and your heart, especially if that negative effect is too strong for you at present. Sometimes taking responsibility for your own grounding and happiness means letting go of someone or putting some kind of space between you and a person in your life who is having too strong a negative effect on you.

Who you are.

The fourth and final part of grounding is in being happy with who you are. It is also, for some, the most difficult. If you are someone who is unhappy in themselves, then the big question is how do I make myself happier with myself. Within the context of this book, the answer can lie in uncovering, understanding, accepting and forgiving those things that happened to cause you to become unhappy in the first place and in correcting any negative beliefs you may have developed about yourself as a result of that unhappiness. This, in short, is what this book is all about and it sets out a successful way of achieving it, especially in the first part: Healing. So, if you are someone who, on reflection, is not really happy in themselves, I invite you to visit or revisit that section of the book.

If, on the other hand, you are not yet ready to face this process or if the process of self-examination and self-healing is proving too difficult, it may be better for you to start with one of the easier-to-achieve aspects of grounding. Look to where you are or to what you do. Start with the external and use the power of grounding and happiness that comes from the external to grow feelings of grounding and happiness in the internal, inside yourself.

This is what I did and the way I did it was to leave behind the life I had at the time and to go away somewhere that was warm and sunny, had lovely beaches, was safe, easy-going and affordable. I chose Thailand. I saved up all I had for one year, which on a UK salary gave me enough to live on for about two years. At the time, it was possible to live in Thailand on around $15 a day. My plan was to stay there for two years, immerse myself in learning Thai massage and then to take it from there. Those two years eventually morphed into eleven and changed my life for ever.

Of all the things I learnt from going away, one was that it takes around three months of being away for the full effects of the life you have been living up to then to begin to fall off you and that the feeling of it falling off you is imperiously wonderful and liberating. More significantly, however, is that it also marks the beginning of no going back. When you have been away from your previous environment for so long, you know you cannot go back fully to being the way you were. The positive feelings you get from changing where you are begin to change who you are.

I know that not everyone is able to do what I did, which was to just pack up and go. At the time I had no family or financial commitments. All I had was my job and my unhappy self. But changing where I was was absolutely necessary to changing who I was and becoming happier with myself. Such a radical step also changed what I was doing and who I was with. It was a really powerful triple positive whammy!

Grounding as in coming back into your body after living partially out of it.

For some people who do not like who they are, where they are, who they are with or what they are doing, they try to get away from their position by cutting themselves off from or escaping from their bodies. They do so because, in most instances, they have no alternative. They are physically unable to walk away from themselves, from where they are, who they are with or what they are doing. Accordingly, they have to find an alternative place, either in their head or in their spirit where they can more easily live and disconnect themselves as much as possible from the aspect of their lives they do not like. Although this is a perfectly understandable way of living, it creates conflict and unhappiness in the part of that person that wants them to be living in their body instead of out of it. In such instances, the way to ground such a person is to help bring them back into their body so they can feel how wonderful it is and how happy it makes them feel. This feeling can then act as a springboard for the person to begin to take the necessary steps to getting themselves back into their body on a more permanent basis. Working with such clients, this is how I achieve that result.

Wearing red to help you ground.

In my healing work, I use a particular energy, or colour, and a specific affirmation when working with out-of-body clients who need grounding. The colour is red. The affirmation is:

It's OK. It's all over. You are safe now.

In energy work, the colour red symbolises the self. It also symbolises family. People who are both strong in themselves and in their connection to their family are said to be strongly red. They are also very grounded and strong in their roots. Red is also, therefore, the colour or energy that symbolises rooting and grounding. People who do not have a strong connection to themselves or to their family are conversely said to be weak in the colour red*.

Red is also the colour of the root chakra**, the energy centre of the body that concerns itself with our most basic survival needs. One of those needs is the need to feel safe. If a person does not feel safe in their environment, they will not go out and integrate themselves into that environment. That environment can be their family home, the school they attend or even their own physical body.

This is why, when working with a client who needs to be grounded through coming back into their body, I use the colour red and the 'you are safe' affirmation. This is how it works.

I invite my client to come in and to lay down on my massage mat in my healing room (I use a mixture of floor-based massage and energy work in my healing work). I then place heavy, red blankets on the parts of their body that root or ground them to the earth. First, their feet, then their lower legs, knees, upper legs and hips. The whole of their body from the hips down. As I lay each blanket on my client I do so with the silent affirmation: 'It's safe here', or 'It's OK. It's all over now, you are safe here' if I know that my client is still in the subconscious pattern of behaviour of trying to protect themselves from a trauma, even though that trauma is now over.

By using the weight of the heavy blankets, I am also metaphysically pushing my client deeper into the floor beneath them, deeper into the earth and thus grounding them. The way my client feels the effect of this is to say how heavy they or their legs feel after the session. Feeling heavy means you are being pulled down into the earth. You are being grounded. I then ask my client how it feels. They almost always say that they really like it and how surprised they are by how good it feels. Some clients are just happy with the feeling but some understand that what I have done is to bring them back into their body and to show them what a positive experience it is.

Seeing the positive, grounding effects that the colour red and heavy, red blankets are having on a client, I sometimes suggest to them that they buy some heavy, red blankets of their own and use them on their sofa or bed at home. Additionally, I suggest wearing the colour red on the lower half of their body, as in, for example, red shoes, red socks, red trousers or a red skirt. The wearing of red clothes on the lower half of your body acts to create red energy in your energy field, enabling a stronger connection to your roots and to the earth, through your feet, thus helping you ground.

* For more information about colour, the energetic properties of colour and the healing effects of colour, please read my book *Emotion and Healing in the Energy Body* (pages 216–237).

** For more information about the chakras, their functions

and characteristics, please see the Appendix section at the back of this book.

Grounding as in sending your energy down into the earth.

A more traditional understanding of grounding can be seen in the practice of going into nature and making a connection between you and the earth, through for example, hugging a tree or sitting down in a field with your back against a tree and through that connection with the tree, sending your energy down into the earth to the centre of the earth. This is grounding as a flow of energy as opposed to grounding as a state of mind (being happy with everything in your life). Both work although usually in the overall process of self-healing following acute or chronic adversity, grounding as a flow of energy precedes grounding as a state of mind.

Grounding as a flow of energy vs. grounding as a state of mind.

For years, I understood grounding to be the process of connecting to the earth and sending the energies of your hurts to its centre, for it was that this use of grounding was to help you let go the energies of your past.

This practice, however, also secretly works to connect you to yourself. Although the initial act is to connect yourself to the centre of the earth so you can ground yourself in it, once established, that connection then mirrors itself back to you. That is the nature of connection. Connection is two-way. It is never one-way. The result is that although you set out to connect yourself to an external thing, the connection then reflects back to you from the external thing, resulting in you connecting yourself to yourself, ultimately in you connecting yourself to your heart. And when you connect or reconnect yourself to your heart, what you feel is enormous happiness, which is why, in the long run, the initial act of grounding is about working towards happiness, attaining grounding is attaining happiness and being grounded is about being happy.

The connection between grounding, happiness, manifestation and abundance.

What is important to realise is that abundance, just like grounding, is a state of mind. It is not a flow. It is neither you wishing for abundance, which is the flow of energy from you (the internal) towards your chosen symbol of abundance (the external), nor you being open to receiving abundance, which is the flow of energy from the external to the internal but instead is a state of mind abundance. It is you connecting to your own abundance. So, in order to aid abundance in your life, you need to develop a state of mind that reflects abundance. In this way, the external (the better life you wish to manifest for yourself) becomes a reflection, or a projection of the internal (your feeling of being in a better life) and the more you strengthen the internal, the more you create the external. It is the same as the way in which you turn your life from an externalised state of victimhood to an internalised state of empowerment through self-healing and self-love, as outlined in the first part of this book. The better you feel about yourself, the internal, the better your life becomes, the external.

And so it is in the relationship between abundance and grounding and grounding and happiness. The more grounded you are, the happier you are and the happier you are, the more abundant you are.

Similarly, the more grounded you are, the stronger you become and the stronger you become the more easily you are able to manifest (in practical terms). Everything is interconnected.

A powerful visualisation to help you ground yourself.

Regardless of wherever you are on your journey toward grounding, here is a powerful visualisation you can do to help ground yourself more strongly.

Imagine, in your mind, the faces of you, your father and your father's parents all at the same time. This is the male side of your family. Hold the images of the three generations in your mind for as long as you can, the longer the better. Imagine them in the right side of your head, or in the right side of your body. This works to open and strengthen the flow of energy through the right side of your body, the male side of your body, strengthening your ability to ground yourself through the right side of your body.

This exercise also works to strengthen your connection to the male side of your family and through that connection to the male side of your own self, to the male you.

Similarly, imagine the faces of you, your mother and your

mother's parents all at the same time. This is the female side of your family. Hold the images of all three generations in the left side of your head, or in the left side of your body, for as long as you can. This works to open and strengthen the flow of energy through the left side of your body, the female side of your body, strengthening your ability to ground yourself through the left side of your body.

This exercise also works to strengthen your connection to the female side of your family and through that connection to the female side of your own self, to the female you.

Doing the exercises one after the other works first to strengthen your connection to your own inner male side and then to your own inner female side, whereas doing both exercises simultaneously connects you to both sides at the same time. In other words, all of you. In the end, the exercise works to connect you to yourself, in the same way as grounding your energy to the centre of the earth does.

The left side/female side and right side/male side symmetry in your body applies when you are a right-handed person. It is the reverse when you are left-handed, so if you are left-handed, you have to place the male side of your family in the left side of your head and in the left side of your body and the female side of your family in the right side of your head and in the right side of your body. This is a generalisation, however, not a rule. It applies in most cases, but not all. There are exceptions. So, if it doesn't work for you the way it is described, don't worry.

Summary.

One of the ways of helping you successfully manifest what you want in life is in removing all the obstacles that can get in your way of manifesting what you want and that is what this section of the book helps you do.

This list of potential obstacles to manifestation serves as a checklist, similar to the start checklist an aeroplane cockpit crew go through before they switch the engines on and ready themselves for take-off. By going through it, it helps you uncover and remove any issues that may block your path towards manifestation. Once you have removed the obstacles, it means you no longer have to be as proactive in your efforts to manifest. Manifestation becomes easier because you have taken away all the things that have gotten in its way.

Practicalities.

I. The law of attraction.

We are born attractors. It is our nature to attract. Although we cannot normally see or feel the process of attraction working within us, we can often experience its consequences. How often have you heard someone say: "Why do I always attract the same type of situation/partner into my life?" Don't forget, it's not only the bad we attract, we attract the good too. We attract everything.

Certain individuals, such as energy workers, shamans or spiritual healers can see the law of attraction at work within us. It is seen as the flow of a particular type of energy, known as subtle energy, into, out of and around our bodies.

This energy flow is most easily seen around certain areas of our bodies known as chakras. It is widely recorded in literature that the flow of energy towards a chakra appears counter-clockwise in form, as in following the direction of the figure 6 from the outside in. This is the flow of energy as it is being drawn from your environment into your body through one of your chakras. Think of it as the flow of air around the base of a tornado. Everything is sucked in from its surrounding environment. This is the law of attraction.

Sometimes, however, the flow appears clockwise, as in the direction of the figure 9, flowing from the inside out. This is the release of energy from your body, through one of your chakras into your environment. This is your body's natural process of letting go.

We have six chakras in our bodies (and one outside our body above our head) and when all are working at the same time to draw in energy from our environment, we become very powerful attractors. Interestingly, when any three of our six bodily chakras are drawing energy into themselves, as in the process of attraction, the visual representation of such energy flow is in the form of three sixes: 666.

What you attract to yourself depends on what you have learnt to attract. It's a bit like learning language. If you have mixed parentage, say English and Spanish, then you probably have learnt fluent English and Spanish at home and you will have no problems with English and Spanish for the rest of your life. They come naturally to you.

Similarly, if you have been surrounded by goodness at home during your growing years, then goodness becomes what you learn to attract in adulthood as goodness is all there ever has been in your environment to learn about. You have no problems with goodness and goodness comes naturally to you. You actually have difficulty attracting adversity. It is a bit like having never taken drugs in your life and one night you are invited to a friend's house party where some people who you don't know take drugs are discreetly taking drugs and yet you don't notice it. You don't see the signs. The signs don't attract you and you don't attract them. It's just not you.

Similarly, if you have been surrounded by tough circumstances, then tough circumstances become what you learn to attract. But just because you have been surrounded by adversity, it doesn't mean that adversity is your lot for the rest of your life. You can change what you attract and you can change it the same way you would learn a new language.

Let's say that after a life of English and Spanish, you want to start speaking Italian. You can buy study books and audio books, watch or download online tutorials, go to evening classes, weekend classes, take private lessons or even leave home for a while to spend some time in Italy, on a student exchange programme, for example.

The same process applies to learning how to attract the good after a life of attracting the bad. There are many wonderful advice and self-help books and online presentations filled with positive and empowering stories, advice, insight, wisdom, suggestion and affirmation. You can take group classes in self-improvement, such as yoga, dance, art, meditation or one of the martial arts. You can work one-on-one with a teacher, mentor or life coach as I did and, of course, you can go away for a while to a good place and surround yourself with good people, which I can also heartily recommend. The more you expose yourself to the good and to the positive, the more you get used to them, to how they work and to how they feel. The more you get used to how they work and to how they feel, the more natural they become to you. And the more natural they become to you, the more naturally they will come to you and the more naturally will you be able to attract them to you.

11. Trusting the universe.

"Trust the universe and everything will work out" and Plan B for when "Trust the universe and everything will work out" doesn't.

For years, when someone told me "just trust the universe and everything will work out", all I wanted to do was thump them.

Trust the universe works when you are in a position of trust, when you have placed your trust in everything all your life and nothing has happened to you to change that. If, however, your trust has been betrayed and especially if you have been badly betrayed by someone who was in a position of trust in your life, such as a parent, family member, teacher or priest, then you are no longer open to trust. You no longer trust in trust and instead you believe, from experience, that there is a chance that something hurtful will happen if you open yourself to trust, so you don't. The result is that you now don't believe in it strongly enough when someone says "trust the universe and everything will work out". As a piece of advice, it's useless. It won't work. You need something else. You need an alternative. You need a Plan B.

Plan B, for me, was 'discover your destiny'. Discovering your destiny works and it works for a number of reasons. First, it reveals to you the thing you should be doing in life. The thing that is right for you. This is priceless information. Instead of just blindly 'putting it out to the universe' and waiting for something to happen, you have something to focus on and work towards, a direction. Second, you can trust it. You can trust it because it comes from the part of you that knows what is right for you, the part of you that has always known what is right for you. Even if you have subsequently lost contact with that part of you, it is still there waiting for you to find it again. It is the destiny you chose for yourself. To help make it work for you, you even organised for help to be given to you along the way. Help, either in spiritual form, as from your spiritual family and friends, or help in real world form, as in help from certain key people you have chosen to meet along your life path, such as a teacher, mentor, friend, co-worker, therapist or healer. Someone who ends up playing an important role in discovering who you are and in keeping you on that path.

So, when you discover and reconnect to your destiny, you also reconnect to all this help. Help actually ends up coming to you from the universe, as some of it comes to you from people who are no longer alive, from people you communicate with through the mediums of prayer, meditation and dreams or through the services of a clairvoyant. So, the third reason why 'discover your destiny' works is the most ironic reason of all: because help comes to you from the universe. Maybe not the kind of help or universe as you would have first imagined either of them to be but help and the universe nevertheless. Help you can trust.

Discovering your destiny brings you to the same point of "trust the universe and everything will work out", but instead of trusting the universe on the advice of someone else, you trust the universe on the advice of yourself.

III. Making it happen.

From asking for help through prayer or meditation or through working with someone trained in the spiritual arts can come the first glimpse of what is right for you to be doing in your lifetime, such as the 'healing with purple' revelation I got when working with my teacher in Chiang Mai. This glimpse, once revealed to you, stays with you, growing and developing in you until it forms a clearer, more realistic and more attainable idea. This clearer idea can come to you spontaneously, any time, either in a dream in the middle of the night, in an idea that comes to you in an unguarded moment of quiet or in an inspirational idea you get first thing when you wake up in the morning. A clearer idea which gives you something to focus on and work towards. With this information, you are now in a position to manifest. First, you discover through your spiritual side what you should be doing. Now you engage your conscious mind side, your ego, to help you manifest it. Now you ask yourself "How do I make it happen?"

This is the process of asking spirit for guidance and then using the ego to put that guidance into action. Manifesting inspirational ideas into concrete projects. Spirit cannot do this by itself. It needs the help of your ego and this is why, when it comes to successfully manifesting your hopes and your dreams, you don't just leave it to the universe, you don't just leave it to prayer or to God. You get up off your backside and make it happen with the tools your ego provides: your ability to write down an idea, research its market potential, develop a business plan, set a goal and a time frame and then when the time is right, execute your dream, which is now a concrete plan. If you need help in turning your dream into a plan, get it. Ask a friend, a neighbour or even a work colleague if they have any ideas or advice to help you shape your goal. Seek out people who have a positive attitude in life or who have achieved or built something concrete for themselves. Maybe you can find a local business mentor or incubator. Visit a trade fair specialising in the new lifestyle, or career you are wanting to manifest. See how it is done. See how other people do it. Successfully. Surround yourself with as many positive people as possible. People who will constantly tell you: "Go ahead and do it. What's stopping you. Just do it". In the company of such people, your body will scoop up, or attract their positive energy, just like the tornado scooping up everything from around itself. The law of attraction. These people will inspire you further and drive you to follow your dream. And, of course, there are inspirational books, online tutorials and motivational speakers available to further help and guide you along your way.

A dream only stays a dream if all you ever do is to keep it in your head. So, take the first step. Get out a sheet of paper, write down what you want to do and then what you have to do in order to turn what you want to do into a reality. In the end, manifestation, in practical terms, is just like anything else. You have to want it enough to get it.

IV. Everyone gets a second chance.

One of the great secrets I have learnt from life is that everyone gets a second chance. Everyone. Everyone gets a second chance to have the life they have always wanted, the way they originally chose it for themselves to be. Everyone gets a second chance to fulfil their destiny.

From personal experience and from my experience of working with others, this second chance presents itself to you around the age of fifty.

Almost everyone on earth spends the first half of their lives living their lives in accordance with the ways and expectations of others. You do what your parents tell you. You do what your school tells you. You do what your employer tells you. You do what society expects of you. You do what your spouse asks of you. You do what your children need of you.

If you have been happy with this and if everything has worked out well enough for you, then you have no need to change anything.

If, however, you are unhappy with how your life has turned out, if for instance the burden of your family has been more than you hoped for, then life gives you a second chance of a fresh start.

This is how it works. You spend roughly the first thirty to forty years of your life living your life unquestioningly and in not seeing the bigger picture. You have, however, ended up unhappy. Things have not worked out the way you would have liked them to have and so you begin to wonder why. Maybe you get the feeling that something is missing, so you start searching for that missing something, or maybe you start looking for the answers as to why your life has ended up the way it has. If there has been a lot of adversity in your life, it can take up to fifteen years to open all the wounds, clean everything out, stitch everything up and get yourself back to where you should be. It can be hard work but what is left is a fresh start, a new and healed life, ready for you to start living it around the age of fifty. It's the chance to start again.

Fifty years may seem like a long time to wait, but if you look after yourself well, you can then have a great run of thirty to thirty-five years of wonderful living.

For some people, the best years of their lives are their early years. For others, it is their later years. That's just the way it is. So, when you have the chance, take it. You've earned it.

Summary.

My wish in sharing all these stories and insights with you is to show you that it is possible to find your way again after a period of adversity or directionlessness and that by finding your path, manifestation and abundance follow. Who you choose to help you find your way is your own free choice. The correct help came my way from people who were not professionally qualified doctors or therapists. I received my first set of guidance from working with my energy teacher, my second set of guidance from doing meditation and my third set of guidance from a channelled-automatic writer.

It is up to you whether you want to better yourself or not and it is up to you whether you want to do what is necessary for you to manifest your wants or not. Sometimes the process takes time. You may need a little patience. You may need a little help. Sometimes it involves going through inconveniences, frustrations, changes, or stages of development before you can finally start your journey. But once you ask for it, once you sincerely ask for it, it will be given to you. Of that, there is no doubt.

Closing words from Jesus Christ.

Over the years I have seen and spoken with many people, both dead and alive in my dreams and meditations. Mostly my mother, my nana, my grandad and my guardian angel, but once, in June 2014, I received some words of advice from Jesus Christ. Just two lines. Nothing more. But two beautiful lines which make the perfect closing words for this book:

Be thankful and
Be gentle to those in pain.

A note of thanks from the author.

Finally, may I say 'Thank you' to you, the reader, for purchasing this book and for taking the time and effort to read it. I hope you have found it of use and of value.

If you have enjoyed reading it, I would be most grateful if you would visit the book's page on Amazon.com and leave a review or a star rating in the customer review section.

In addition to my writing, I also give workshops on energy work and spiritual healing and offer one-to-one healing sessions. Details can be found on my homepage at: www.roberthenderson.at

With thanks and best wishes to all,

Robert Henderson.

Other books by the same author.

Emotion and Healing in the Energy Body. (Healing Arts Press, 2015).

A comprehensive guide to subtle energy and its associated physical manifestations in the body, detailing the characteristics and properties of eight different types of energy: Emotional, Mental, Spiritual, Sexual, Environmental, Interpersonal, Ancestral and Karmic.

The book additionally explains how suffering acute emotional trauma or long-term stress causes negative energies to accumulate in the body much like fat deposits. Our physical body reacts to these energetic build-ups, or blockages, leading to physical conditions such as pain and weakness in the joints, digestive distress and persistent tension in certain areas of the body, such as the shoulders. The book describes 30 such bodily ailments, detailing their exact location and specific physical characterisation, such as an area of tightness, tension, contraction, inflammation or stagnation and explains the energetic cause of each one. Finally, the book shows that physical ailments caused by the energies of past or current emotional hurt can be released and healed through massage and yoga, allowing your body to return to its natural state of freedom and health.

You can purchase the book here:
https://www.amazon.com/dp/1620554275/

Appendix.

The chakras.

Throughout this book I make much reference to chakras. In case you are unfamiliar with chakras, here is a short overview and explanation of them.

Chakras are energy centres in your body, lying a centimetre or two underneath the surface of your skin, through which you absorb and use energy from your environment, for example the energy you work in while at your place of work. This is energy you neither eat, drink nor inhale. It is energy you absorb, like energy from the sun. It comes in through your skin and gets absorbed into your body.

The energy absorbed by your chakras is used to develop your emotional, mental and spiritual growth, as opposed to your physical growth. It can, however, have a physical effect in your body. For example, if your work environment is a stressful place to be in, the energy you absorb into your body from being in that stressful environment creates a parallel physical stress in your body, manifesting as tightness in the muscles around your solar plexus, mid-back, shoulders (trapezius) and lower jaw. If you are sensitive to the energy of stress in your workplace, you might even notice your body physically tighten as you approach your place of work in the morning. This is the connection between environmental energy, as absorbed by your chakras, and the physical condition of your body.

Environmental energy, once absorbed into your body through one of your chakras, is then distributed around your body via energy channels, known as meridians. It is similar in function to the distribution of blood around your body through your veins and arteries.

You have six chakras located in your body.

The first is located in the area of your perineum. Its function is to absorb and use the energy from your earliest environment, from where you live following your birth. It also absorbs the energy of the people living with you in that environment, such as your parents and siblings (if you have any).

The second is located just below your navel. Its function is to absorb and use the energies from the environments you spend time in during your childhood. This can be from your family home, for example, but also from kindergarten, playschool, early school, playgrounds and other places where you go to play with your friends. Everywhere you go to between the ages three to eleven, thereabouts.

The third is located in the area of your solar plexus. Its function is to absorb and use the energies from your later educational environments, from ages eleven to around twenty-two, from your places of work and from social gatherings.

The fourth is located to the right of your heart, on your sternum. Its function is to absorb and use the energies from all your experiences of love during life.

The fifth, located in the front of your throat and the sixth, located between your eyebrows, absorb and use the energy from your spiritual environments, such as when you are in a room full of people doing meditation, or if you ever attend a lecture by a renowned spiritual person, such as His Holiness the Dalai Lama.

You also have a seventh chakra, located above your head. It lies outside the realm of your physical body and doesn't absorb anything from your physical environment. It contains 'the light' and if you connect to it with your conscious mind, you can feel yourself ascending into a state of 'beyond mind' where there are no thought or emotional processes.

Although chakras are described as being linked to certain stages of development in your life, such as the first chakra being linked to the stage of your development at home with your family following your birth, once they are awakened, they stay active until death. Your first chakra will still be affected by your connection to your family even when you are ninety-nine!

The connection between your chakras and the condition of your physical body.

The quantity and quality of environmental energy absorbed and stored in each of your six bodily chakras determines the condition of your physical body in and around the area surrounding each of those six chakras. For instance, if your first chakra, located in the area of your perineum, is tight, then the area of your body surrounding your first chakra: your adductors, pelvic girdle, glutes and the tops of your hamstrings will be similarly tight, physically tight.

What is a tight chakra?

Think, for a moment, of any of your chakras as being like your stomach. The function of a chakra is to absorb and process environmental energy. The function of your stomach is to absorb and process nutritional energy, in the form of food. When your stomach has had the right amount of the right food, it is happy. When it hasn't had enough food, it becomes unhappy. When your stomach has had too much of one particular type of food or too much of an unhealthy food, it also becomes unhappy and sends you distress signals. You feel it in your body. It is the same with your chakras. They can be happy or unhappy and they send you signals when they are in distress.

A happy chakra is one which has had a very satisfying experience. Take, for example, your heart chakra. If you have been lucky in love throughout your life, your heart chakra will be in a state of happiness from all the energy of love it has absorbed. Your heart chakra and the areas of your body surrounding your heart chakra: your chest, lungs, upper back, shoulders and arms will be similarly happy. They will be in good health and full of vitality. They will generally feel warm to your touch and the muscles, fascia and connective tissue will be soft, flexible and strong.

An unhappy heart chakra, on the other hand, is one that hasn't had enough love or has had too much of a particular unhealthy experience, such as grief or loneliness. An unhappy chakra reveals its distress to you by being in one of three states: weak, tight or cold. Let's continue with your heart chakra by means of further explanation.

If you haven't had any love in your life, or maybe not enough love, then your heart chakra, which absorbs all the energy of love from those experiences, will be empty, just like an empty stomach.

It hasn't been fed enough. As a result of being underfed, your heart chakra and the areas of your body surrounding your heart chakra will become weak. They will lack vitality. The muscles, fascia and connective tissue will be weak, such as muscular weakness in your chest and upper back and an empty heart, just like an empty stomach, will cause you to ache.

What can also happen when you have not had enough love in your life is that you become angry at not having had enough love in your life. This can be a very subtle process and you may not always feel it, especially if you started to receive insufficient love from a very early age in your life. In adulthood, you can become completely unaware of how angry you have become as a result of this. Anger is an energy which causes your body to tighten – think how you or your body feels when someone at work makes you mad with their annoying behaviour – and a chakra that has not received sufficient energy will become angry at not having received sufficient energy and will tighten. If you have been unlucky in love and you have not received enough love in your life, there will be a resulting anger in your heart chakra at this experience. This anger will make your heart chakra and the areas of your body surrounding your heart chakra tight. Muscles, fascia and connective tissue will be physically tight.

The third state of distress is coldness. Certain life experiences create coldness in your body. These are the experiences of lovelessness (a life without love), loneliness, sadness, loss, grief and fear. There is nothing wrong with a little bit of fear or a little bit of loneliness in your life. Everyone experiences them. Too much fear or loneliness, however, creates too much coldness in your body and when your body is too cold, it finds it more difficult to function healthily.

Coldness creates contraction in your body. Think how you

contract yourself in order to keep your inner self warm when you are in a very cold environment. So, going back to your heart, if, for example, you have experienced a lot of sadness in your life, your heart chakra will have absorbed this cold energy into itself and this coldness will correspondingly form as physical coldness in the body areas surrounding your heart chakra, most notably in the soft tissue between your breasts and your clavicles. Some people who have experienced acute grief or sadness find upper lung breathing difficult, because the intercostal muscles are in a state of contraction due to the coldness of the grief or sadness stored there.

Oftentimes you can go to your doctor with a pain in your chest or in your arms. Your doctor will do tests. You may even be sent to hospital for additional tests. But the tests come back clear. The tests say you are fine, yet your body is in distress. This is because your pain is not medical, it is energetic. Taking the example of your heart again, if you have been unfortunate enough to have received very little or no love in your life and this has gone on to create sadness and loneliness in you and maybe some anger too at not being sufficiently loved, then your heart, your heart chakra and the areas of your body close to your heart chakra; your chest, lungs, upper back, shoulders and arms will be affected by a complex mixture of physical tightness and tension, coldness and contraction and emptiness and weakness. Such bodily pain reveals the link between your emotional environment, your energetic environment and the condition of your physical body.

This is why accepting and understanding your chakras, or energy centres, is useful to your overall wellness. By accepting and understanding the link between physical pain and your current or past energetic environments, you can work to release physical pain from your body through the release of the energy causing that physical pain from the chakra in your body which is closest to the area of the physical pain, for example the release of physical pain from your pectorals, deltoids, triceps and upper arms through the release of energy from the energy centre closest to these body areas, your heart chakra.

Western medicine is sceptical of chakras because chakras cannot be measured by western medicine approved measuring devices. Nor can they be seen when you open up a body for a post-mortem examination. There is also a resistance among some people to accepting the existence of chakras because of the word used to describe them. Chakra is a Sanskrit word and is therefore regarded by some as applying to Indian culture only, especially Indian religious culture, Hinduism, and Hindu-related health practices, such as yoga or Ayurveda. Environmental energy and how the human body reacts to it is universal, regardless of where you live and what words are used to describe the process.

This section on the chakras is designed to give you, the reader, a brief overview of the subject. If you would like to learn more about chakras, what they look like, what they feel like, their functions and purposes and the effect they have on your physical body and on your wider wellness, I invite you to read my first book: *Emotion and Healing in the Energy Body* (Healing Arts Press, 2015).

The effects of past or current emotional hurt in your body.

There are two types of pain you can feel in your body: physical pain and metaphysical, or *energetic* pain.

Physical pain is the type of pain that when you poke your finger into it, it makes you go "Ouch!". Physical pain is the result of some sort of physical damage that has happened to your body, such as a break, crack, fracture, pull, strain, rupture, tear, cut, graze or bruise. It can also be as a result of infection or disease in your body.

Metaphysical pain, on the other hand, doesn't make you go ouch when you put your finger into it. Indeed, even putting your finger into it can prove difficult as energetic pain is not always easy to pinpoint. You know you have a pain in your body because you can feel it, yet when you try to pinpoint its actual location by pointing to it, you find you cannot. What can also happen is that when you do put your finger on the part of your body where you feel your pain, the pain inexplicably disappears. It is suddenly not there. It is as if you can feel the pain in your mind but not with your physical touch. Some doctors accordingly call this pain psychosomatic pain or pain that is in your head. This is both incorrect and unfair.

Metaphysical pain is not as a result of direct injury or disease. It is as a result of non-contact injury or disease, such as being forced to live in an environment of fear, shame, humiliation, terror, deprivation, neglect, anger and hatred, or in an environment where you have been disempowered, dominated or controlled.

The physical, bodily after-effects of living in such environments are not psychosomatic or in your head. They are real. Very real. Physical pain, tightness, weakness, coldness, contraction, agitation and even organ dysfunction. Most western doctors can see them and even palpate them yet cannot properly diagnose them. This is because the prognosis is in your energy body, not your physical body and most western doctors are simply not trained in energy body diagnosis and treatment.

On the other hand, doctors trained in native medicine, such as shamans, or in eastern medicine, such as doctors of Traditional Chinese Medicine, can and do diagnose and treat pain held in the energetic system.

Metaphysical/energetic pain can affect you in almost any part of your body. To find out exactly where, visit a Shiatsu therapist or a clinic where Traditional Chinese Medicine (TCM) is practised.

When you visit a TCM clinic, one of the things you will probably see on the walls of the clinic is a set of western anatomical charts of the human body, front and back, onto which have been transposed the eastern system of energy lines and energy points, called meridians and acupuncture points, which make up the composition of your energy system. Study these charts. You can also find smaller versions of them on the internet. If you have pain in your abdomen that your western doctor cannot diagnose, for example, look at a TCM chart showing the abdominal area of the body and see if the location of your pain corresponds to any of the acupuncture points shown on the chart. This may not reveal the exact location or nature of your pain but it is a start. For example, if you have a pain in your stomach and you look at a chart you may see that the area of your pain corresponds roughly to the location of some acupuncture points in the abdominal area of the body which are called Stomach 23, Stomach 24 and Stomach 25. It is not important to know what Stomach 23, 24 and 25 mean, it is only important that you know their names and general location. Armed with this information, you can then visit a doctor of Traditional Chinese Medicine and tell them that you think you have a pain in your abdomen, in or around the area of Stomach 23–25. Let the doctor then take it from there. If indeed your abdominal pain is a physical pain relating to an energetic pain located in the region of those three acupuncture points, the TCM doctor will be able to treat you more quickly and more effectively than a doctor of western medicine.

The reason why I bring attention to the energy body is because all the emotional, mental and energetic effects of any period of abuse you may have had to live through are stored in your energetic body, in the form of energy, and because what you went through was possibly very painful, the effect of that energy stored in your energy body will cause you some degree of parallel pain in your physical body, as both bodies, your energy and your physical body, are interconnected. To ignore the existence of your energy body is to ignore the origin of much of the physical pain you can experience in your body. Pain which, because western doctors are often unable to diagnose properly, is labelled nonspecific body pain or psychosomatic pain.

What does emotional or energetic pain feel like?

The answer depends on which emotion or energy it is. Think for a moment how different it is to feel afraid than it is to feel angry.

Fear commonly causes people to shut down. When you shut

down, you do not move. You do not speak, you do not eat, you do not look other people in the eye. You can feel heavy, without energy and you may want to go to sleep for a long time. Fear is also a cold energy. It causes you to feel internal cold, to shiver or to sweat cold sweat and when your body is cold, it contracts. So, two of the most noticeable physical effects of the energy of fear are that it causes your body to feel cold and it causes the muscles and connective tissue in the area of the cold to contract and stiffen.

Anger, on the other hand, makes you need to get up and move about. You cannot lie still and be angry. When you are angry, you get tense and agitated. The energy of anger makes your muscles tighten and harden, especially in the areas of your stomach, mid-back, trapezius and jaw. When your stomach is tight, you cannot eat. Physical tightness in these areas of your body is as a result of anger, frustration, or impatience that have been building up in your body and which are as a result of you having to spend time in an environment that has been making you angry, frustrated or impatient, such as at work, or at home.

Very old emotional pain that has been stored in your body for many years, such as unprocessed emotional pain from early childhood or infancy, can cause chronic or acute distress in certain parts of your body in adulthood, especially very close to the running of your spine on both sides, the areas of your lower back around L3–S1 and the sacroiliac joint. Similar physical pain can also be felt in the tops of your hamstrings, deep in your abdomen, close to your navel and in and around your sexual organs. By the time such pains appear in adulthood, the person experiencing them has often lost all recollection of their childhood and infancy and so never connects childhood emotional pain with physical pain in adulthood. Accordingly, when the pain arises, the treatment sought is medical instead of energetic.

Where do you store emotional or energetic pain in your body?

Emotions, in their energetic form, such as the energy of fear, the energy of anger or the energy of love, are stored in your energy system. They are primarily stored in specific parts of your energy system called chakras but are additionally carried around your body along the energy meridians which are paired to the chakra where the particular emotional energy is primarily stored. The energy of fear, for example, which is primarily stored in your second chakra (the area of your body between your navel and the top of your pubis) is carried around your body by the meridian paired to the second chakra: the kidney meridian. So, in order to understand where the emotional energy of fear is stored in your body, you need to know the locations of your second chakra and your kidney meridian and then map both onto a western anatomical chart of the body. This will show you where the energy of fear can be found in your body and so which areas of your body can be affected by the energy of fear.

Fear, of course, isn't the only emotional energy we store in our bodies. There are many others. So, to help you, here is a short overview of the different emotional energies we hold in our bodies, which chakras we store them in, along which energy channels they are carried and which parts of the body are affected by them. For ease of description purposes, I have organised the overview by chakra.

1. Emotions and feelings stored in your first chakra.

There are three: shame, humiliation and disgust. They are housed close to the base of your torso, in your pelvic girdle, wrapped around your bottom two sacral vertebrae and tailbone.

Shame and humiliation are the emotions and feelings which, if you do not process and let go, cause the most damage to your life, especially humiliation. They are also the exception to the chakra-meridian rule in as much as they are not carried around your body by any energy meridian.

The energy that creates feelings of safety is also to be found in your first chakra. This energy comes from being picked up and held around your hips by your parents when you were a toddler. Adults lacking a feeling of safety in life can find themselves unable to integrate fully into life and to fully fulfil their wants and desires. In energy work, one of the ways to heal a lack of feeling safe in a person is to place your hands on their hips while silently imparting the message: You are safe.

2. Emotions and feelings stored in your second chakra.

There are four: joy, excitement (anticipation), fear and repulsion. They are stored in your lower abdominal area, your lower back between L4–L2 and in your kidneys. They are carried around your body by the meridian paired to the second chakra, the kidney meridian. Although emotions like fear and excitement may appear to be totally different, they are actually formed of the same energy which is why, in some people, fear and excitement are very strongly interconnected.

The energies that create the feelings of being reassured and of being supported also belong in your second chakra. These feelings come from being hugged or held closely by your parents in your childhood, especially if you ever got a fright or had a bad dream or if you ever had a bad day at school and you needed some support to keep you going. Adults lacking the feelings of being supported or reassured can also find themselves unable to integrate fully into life or to fully fulfil their wishes. In energy work, the way to heal a lack of support or reassurance in someone is to hold them in almost the same way a parent would hold their child during or following a difficult or frightening experience and to silently impart the message: It's OK. I've got you. Everything is going to be OK.

3. Emotions and feelings stored in your third chakra.

There are many and like the emotions and feelings of the first and second chakras, some can be labelled as 'positive', while others can be labelled as 'negative', although, in truth, they are all neutral, as they are all just energy. Some just happen to create a pleasant reaction in your body, others an unpleasant one.

Of the 'positive' emotions and feelings stored in the third chakra, the more noticeable ones include confidence, courage, will and determination and the senses of achievement and pride in your efforts.

Of the 'negative' emotions and feelings stored in your third chakra, the more noticeable ones include anxiety, aggression, anger, frustration, impatience, cruelty, envy and (the need to) control.

All these emotional energies and feelings are stored in your upper abdominal area, your mid-back and in your stomach, spleen, liver and gallbladder. They are carried around your body by the meridians paired to the third chakra: the stomach, spleen, liver and gallbladder meridians.

The emotions and feelings of the third chakra are also said to be of the air element. This is why, when certain of the negative third chakra emotional energies, such as anger, build up and then release inside you, it is the same as air pressure building up in a balloon until it bursts. This is why you can sometimes explode with anger.

Although emotions such as anger and frustration are located in the upper abdominal area of your body, their energy is also carried around your body by the gallbladder meridian. If you check the running of the gallbladder meridian on a TCM gallbladder meridian chart, you will see that the meridian runs up the side of your head, which is why when you get angry or frustrated or impatient, you sometimes also get a headache. This is the gallbladder meridian carrying air energy into your head, causing pressure to build there, which you then feel as headache. This is another classic example of the connection between emotional energy and bodily physical discomfort.

4. Emotions and feelings stored in your fourth chakra.

Again, there are many and as with all other emotions and feelings, some can be classified as being nice, while others are not so nice!

Of the nicer emotions and feelings stored in your fourth chakra, the major ones include love, trust, tolerance, acceptance, openness, letting go and forgiveness. These are warming energies.

Of the not so nice emotions and energies stored in your fourth chakra, the major ones include sadness, grief, loss, despair, hopelessness, loneliness and lovelessness (a life without love). These are cooling energies.

All these emotions and feelings are stored in your upper chest cavity, upper back, shoulders, lungs, heart, arms and hands. They are carried around your body by the energy meridians paired to the fourth chakra: the lung, large intestine, small intestine, heart, pericardium and triple heater meridians. When the energy being carried in these meridians is one of the warming energies, it causes the body areas surrounding these meridians to be similarly warm, open, vital and strong. When the energy is cold, it causes everything to cool, contract and stiffen.

5. Emotions and feelings stored in your fifth and sixth chakras.

There are none. However, the areas of your body which are

directly influenced by the condition of your fifth and sixth chakras, your throat and your head, can be affected by emotions from other chakras which are being carried in meridians running through your throat and your head. For example, you can feel the effects of fear, which belongs to your second chakra, in the base of your throat. In this example, the energy of fear is being carried in the kidney meridian which runs up the front of your body through the base of your throat, so when you have fear energy in your kidney meridian in the area of your throat, it causes the muscles in your throat and neck to cool and contract, causing a restriction in speaking. This happens most noticeably when you are afraid to speak up for yourself, to express yourself freely, usually against someone who is trying to exert control over you.

This section on 'The effects of past or current emotional hurt on your body' is designed to give you, the reader, a brief overview of the subject. If you would like to learn more about energy, the different types of energy and all the effects different types of energy have on the physical body, I invite you to read my first book: *Emotion and Healing in the Energy Body* (Healing Arts Press, 2015).

Index

C

D

E

F

G

H

I

K

L

M

N

P

S

T

www.ingramcontent.com/pod-product-compliance
Ingram Content Group UK Ltd.
Pitfield, Milton Keynes, MK11 3LW, UK
UKHW041954190726
13854UKWH00005B/1970

9 783951 993003